MW01644564

LETTERS

FROM

Sacred Agent 007

LETTERS

FROM

Sacred Agent 007

To Friend Doug,
FOR OLD TIME'S SAKE,
Sacred Agent 007

DUANE WINDEMILLER, PHD

Other Books By the Author
Which Reminds Me: Memoirs of an Octogenarian
Getting To Heaven and Other Homilies

Library of Congress Number: 2006900393
ISBN: Hardcover 1-4257-0744-0
Softcover 1-4257-0743-2

This book was printed in the United States of America.

To order additional copies of this book, contact:
Xlibris Corporation
1-888-795-4274
www.Xlibris.com
Orders@Xlibris.com
33088

CONTENTS

This book is dedicated
to the thousands of
readers around
the country
who have read my letters
and encouraged their
publication.

Blessed be letters—
they are the monitors,
they are also the comforters,
and they are the only true
heart-talkers.

—Donald Grant Mitchell

Preface

I was a chaplain in Korea when Ian Fleming was creating Secret Agent 007 to be released on the world in his novel Casino Royale. Noting the alliterative quality of Secret and Sacred, I jokingly began to call myself Sacred Agent 007. After all, if the Queen needed someone to plot for the overthrow of her enemies, did not God need someone to plot for the overthrow of Satan and his forces?

Out of the army and in Boston University working for my PhD in Psychology, I became the student pastor of the North Congregational Church in Abington, Massachusetts. I often preached to the National Guard troops early on Sunday morning, then, still in uniform, I would rush back to Abington to preach to my congregation there. Entering the pulpit I might say, "Here is Sacred Agent 007 returning from fighting the forces of evil."

About this time I heard an older minister at a conference say, "Preachers spend far too little time on the preparation of the messages in their newsletters. After all, a far higher percentage of the congregation is going to read the newsletter than listen to his sermon on Sunday." This struck the chord of truth and I began to spend a lot more time on my monthly newsletters which I signed—what else—Sacred Agent 007.

I have been doing that through the years, and in this book, Letters from Sacred Agent 007, you will find some of the ones 007 believes you might find enjoyable, educational and inspiring.

The Tiffany Lamp Connection

I heard my mother quote Edwin Markham's quatrain enough times to etch it on my mind and make it a guiding principle of my life.

He drew a circle that shut me out—
Heretic, rebel, a thing to flout.

But Love and I had the wit to win;
We drew a circle that took him in!

Mom grew up knowing at the core of her being that she was a thing to flout. She was born out of wedlock and most of those who knew her felt, like her uncles, that she should be taken into the woods and left to die. Children called her names and wouldn't play with her. She was shunned, a thing to flout. But in her teens she wandered into a church, lured by the strains of *Amazing Grace* and there learned of a man who drew a circle that took her in, Jesus. No one can describe the joy and freedom she felt that night. She ran home and told her mother, my grandmother, and she, too, found that joy. Together they went through life, spreading the gospel of God's all inclusive love.

God, through Jesus, says to us, *Come unto me, all you who are weary*. He didn't say *Come unto me all you who are weary and who believe in the virgin birth, but come unto me, all of you—Protestant, Catholic, Christian, Muslim, Buddhist, infidel, thief on the cross, worker in the vineyard for one hour or a whole day. My grace is all encompassing. It is sufficient for you. It cannot be earned nor can it be measured. My circle is love and it encompasses all humanity.*

So what happened!

Why have Christians cut out the tongues of other Christians, cut off their heads, burned each other on the stake by the hundreds of thousands? If God drew a circle that took everyone in, why are some of us trying to push others of us out? Consider the following story.

Walter Wight was a wonderful young preacher, fresh out of divinity school. He received his call to become a preacher in the church in Abington where I was his pastor. Now he had a parish not far from Bradford and the church I served there. Walter was evangelical. He was eager to save as many souls for the Lord as he could—including mine. He knew my theology and he was fearful that, unless I changed my thinking and beliefs, I might not make it to heaven. One day after some conversation in my study in Bradford I said to him, "Walter, One thing I am certain of—when I go through heaven's gates you will be waiting for me And will you be surprised that I made it, too."

Walter was looking through one of the many colored panes in the great Tiffany Lamp. And it was not the same color pane I looked through.

The bulb inside the Tiffany lamp shed pure white light but Walter and I saw slightly different colors. If a Catholic looks through his colored pane, he will see a different colored light than either Walter or I did. If a Lutheran or Episcopalian looked through his colored pane . . . and so on.

Luther looked through a different color than the Pope did and the reformation ensued. Luther later got married and someone asked him why he did it and he replied, "To spite the Devil and tease the Pope."

We have to look through a colored filter. To look at God directly would mean death. John Wesley looked through a different color than the Church of England, took to the fields, preached to hundreds of thousands and a great new Denomination of Christians was born.

Methodists and Quakers looked through different panels of the lamp. They had very little to do with each other—avoided contact with each other when possible. One day George Fox, the founder of Quakerism, saw a Methodist approaching. The Methodist crossed the street so as to avoid direct contact with Fox. Fox crossed the street, too, and they met in the middle. Fox said, "Does your heart warm within you when I say the name, Jesus?"

The Methodist said, "Yes."

"Me, too," said Fox. "Lets shake." And they shook hands. They understood they were looking through different color panels but at the same God.

God created us all and loves us all. Lets give that infidel over there a little more wiggle room.

Praying With Your Mouth Full

In the comic strip "Sherman On the Mount" the chubby but saintly monk, Brother Sherman, talking with his guardian angel. He complains, "No matter how hard I pray, I still don't lose weight."

The angel replies, "It depends on how you pray, Sherman!"

"What do you mean?" Sherman says.

The angel responds, "It might help if you didn't pray with your mouth full."

Prayer is a two-way street. We have to help God help us. It has been said, "The Gulf Stream can flow through a soda straw if the straw is placed in the right direction. It is a matter of orientation. Sherman's orientation was a little off. We would not want to go to the race track to pray for strength to overcome our gambling addiction. We'd be praying with our mouth full.

A man once came to my study and pleaded with me to intercede with his wife not to leave him. He had broken his vow not to drink again and after many such broken vows she made her decision. I said to him, "As you know, we have an Alcoholics Anonymous meeting every Monday night here in our church basement. If you will meet me there next Monday night, I will agree to talk with your wife." He agreed, but he did not show up at the meeting. He was praying with his mouth full.

I attended the AA meetings from time to time. I found more inspiration there than in many a church meeting. They knew what it was to let go and let God. I told them once I wished I had a Sinners Anonymous upstairs. Too many Christians talk the talk but don't walk the walk. They pray with their mouths full. I found much humor in the AA meetings. One member in his testimony told how he bought a keg of beer and placed it on the coffee table in his living room. He was going to prove to himself that he had licked his problem. He said to the group, "Now after that keg was gone . . ." He was praying with his mouth full.

It might seem strange that God's miracles require our cooperation but it is true. When he gave us freedom he gave us the independence to choose the wrong as well as the right. He gave us the freedom! Freedom has its down side. It costs. It is work. It is cooperation. Hear this parable of the sparrow. A sparrow landed on the edge of another sparrow's nest to pass the time of day. He found the other sparrow in bad condition. It was weak and dying. "What's the matter with you?" asked the visiting sparrow.

"Well," said the sick one, "I heard that God takes care of the sparrows and I'm waiting for him to take care of me—to feed me."

"Ah, but you've got it wrong," said the healthy sparrow. "God did promise to feed us sparrows but he didn't promise to bring the food to the nest."

So, Sherman, you have your work cut out for you. You need exercise and one of the best exercises for losing weight is to put both hands on the edge of the table and push. And while you are pushing—with your mouth empty—pray with all your might. I'll keep reading the comics to see if that fat little tummy gets any smaller. Whether it does or it doesn't, I'll still love you—and I'm sure God will, too.

Making Holes In the Darkness

When Robert Louis Stevenson was a small boy, he was with his family in Paris. One evening his mother came into the room and saw him in the dim light looking out the window. "What are you doing in the dark?"

"I'm watching a man make holes in the darkness." he said. She leaned over his shoulder and looked out and saw a very foggy night. And she saw the lamplighter doing his work. As each light was lit it did seem literally to make a hole in the fog. When I read this I thought, there's a lot of dark in this world and a lot of lamplighters are needed. My next thought was that we are all called to be lamplighters—called by the first lamplighter, Jesus. He said to us ***You** are the light of the world; Let your light shine before men*. Maybe when its time to make resolutions one of the best would be "I may not be a thousand watt bulb but I can be a little candle and make a hole in the darkness for someone."

In today's world we tend to think that unless we can do something big it is not worth doing, but Jesus gave us a different message. He said *even if those around you have many talents and you have only one talent, do not hide it in the ground.*

I thought of this while teaching psychology. The students had to learn the law of JND, just noticeable difference. They probably wished Ernst Weber had kept his findings to himself so they wouldn't have to memorize it all. But whether it is light, sound, color or whatever, it is helpful to know just how much difference will be noticed by our senses. How much light will make a hole in someone's darkness?

A business man was entering his office building when he saw a man with no legs sitting on the sidewalk selling pencils. He said to the man, "You can save me some work. I was going to order pencils today, but I can get them right here. How much would two dozen of them be, sir?" The man told him and the pencils were bought. The next day the doorman brought an envelope to the business man in his office. In it was a letter full of thanks from the pencil-seller. When the business man went by him that day, he said, "It wasn't necessary to thank me. It was just a business deal."

The legless man replied, "I wasn't thanking you for buying the pencils. It was just that you called me **sir**."

Not a great light, probably, but a hole in someone's darkness.

Little things count a lot when it comes to making holes in the darkness.

Like when a mother asked her young son to go out on the patio and bring in the dog's dish. He opened the door a crack and closed it. He went to his father, who was reading the paper, and said, "Will you come with me while I get the dog's dish?"

"The dog's dish isn't very heavy," said his father. "Why do you need me?"

"Because it's too dark to go out without a father," he said, so the two of them went out to bring in the dish. A small hole in the darkness, perhaps, but I'm sure that father got a mark on Heaven's Tally Board. We don't have to go very far to make a hole in the darkness for someone.

Who Can't You Stand?

I have a bone to pick with Will Rogers. He said, "I never met a man I didn't like." I never really believed him. I thought he was, to say the least, ingenuous. After all, even Jesus met people he didn't like. Preaching to the Pharisees once he called them a generation of vipers. And don't give me the line about Jesus really liked the people; he just didn't like what they were doing. That's a copout! Let's be honest. There are people I don't like and I'm not going to perform some kind of spiritual surgery to separate the person from his deeds. Provided we are not multiple personalities, we are what we do!

There are people I don't like whom I can work with and for, and maybe learn to like them in the process, but how about people we can't stand? People we won't be around if we can help it. When I was quite young I saw a neighbor farmer whip his horse till its eyes bulged and it reared and foamed at the mouth. It might have been because the horse bucked while it was being hitched. Talk about "not standing!" I hated that man! If I had been big enough and had a whip, I'd have whipped him like Jesus did the money changers in the temple. I had visions of that horse getting a whip and beating the man. I feel just as revulsed today when I hear on TV of a man abusing his wife and children. I know you're saying, "Why preacher, you should pray for that man." I do, I do—through clenched teeth.

The word *stand* goes way back to the word *stone* from which we get *stink*—to offend the nostrils. I imagine in some distant past a person might say, "I like you personally but I don't want to be close enough to smell you." We are so much more genteel today. If we are in the office and someone we "can't stand" engages us in conversation, we say, "Excuse me. I have an important engagement," and we stop off in the men's room so we won't be lying. That's a trivial example, but I'm sure you can think of some not so trivial.

As Christians don't we have a responsibility to get along with people we can't stand? Yes, but it's a conditional responsibility not an absolute one. The Apostle Paul said so in his letter to the Romans: *As much as possible, for your part, live peaceably with everybody.* I know that "if possible" leaves the door open for all sorts of rationalization, but as I said above, we have to be honest in our hearts about it. I have a rule of thumb: if the person I can't stand is a part of my daily world, yes, I have the responsibility to do *as much as possible to live peaceably with that person.* Let me give you a f'rinstance.

I was working my way through college—American University in Washington, D.C. My job was in the Department of the Interior Cafeteria. I had a woman boss. She made life miserable for every employee. No matter how good a job we did, if there was a short time when we were not working, we were not allowed to rest. She'd find work for us to do. One day she had me polishing the brass strip running across the floor in the dining room. I couldn't "stand" the woman, but pursuant to Paul's advice I tried to live peaceably with her. I began to talk to her about her life, a question here and a question there. She seemed glad to answer them, like it was therapeutic. I discovered she had the most desperate upbringing imaginable: father left before she was born, put out to adoption, living with several families, abused, marrying at sixteen to get out on her own, only to be left pregnant by this man, etc. I began to admire her so much for making something of herself that I couldn't dislike her any more. I didn't even mind polishing that brass strip on the floor! I guess the old adage proved true once again: **the only person we can change is us.** When I understood her, *I* changed, and when I changed, I took her off the list of the persons I couldn't stand. I could stand her because I understood her.

I guess the author of the book of Proverbs knew what he was talking about when he wrote *With all thy getting get understanding.*

But I still believe there are people only God could love. One of those is that horse-beating farmer. I'm giving him to you, God.

Sex

Now that I have your attention lets talk about *sects.* Both "sex" and "sects derive from the Latin, *secare:* (to divide, to cut off. Or as Arthur Guiterman put it so succinctly:

Amoebas at the start
Were not complex;
They tore themselves apart
And started sex.

Asking Guiterman's pardon I did a little substituting:

Churches at the start
Were not complex;
They tore themselves apart
and started sects,

There you have the history of the Christian Church in a nutshell.

It surprised me to discover that in the US alone one new sect forms every week. Can you imagine what Jesus must be thinking about that?

On a trip to Washington DC. I dropped in on a church near the hotel. I knew nothing about its history. The congregation was small, so I stood out like a pygmy in a Celtics uniform. I was startled when the preacher said, looking at me, "There are fourteen people in this city who are going to heaven and I can name every one of them!" That preacher "knew" he had the one true orthodox church in the capital of our country. He was orthodox.

Orthodoxy is made from two Latin words: *ortho* (straight) and *doxy* (belief) or "straight belief." Most sects believe they alone know the "straight truth" or the "real meaning of the Bible." And to be a member, you must believe as they do. This makes some churches difficult to join, as in the following story by the comedian, Eno Phillips.

"I met someone and struck up a conversation. Right away we discovered that our religious backgrounds were very much alike: The new person said, "Are you Protestant or Catholic?"

"Protestant." I said.

"Me too! What type of Protestant?"

"Baptist," I said.

"Baptist!" he said, "Me too! Northern or Southern Baptist?"

"Northern Baptist," I said.

"Me too!" he said. They go back and forth like this for a while and it ends with one saying, "Northern conservative fundamentalist Baptist Great Lakes Region Council of 1879 or Northern conservative fundamentalist Baptist Great Lakes Region Council of 1912?"

"Northern conservative fundamentalist Baptist Great Lakes Region Council of 1912." A knock-down scrap ensues as each cries out, "Heretic!"

I don't know the number of these small "fly-by-night" sects ("fly-by-night" means the sect the other fellow belongs to), but I have a deep conviction that Jesus would not approve. Even the shape of the cross has him with open arms. *Come unto me*, he said, *all ye who labor and are heavy laden and I will give you rest*. He did not say, *Come unto me all ye who are weary and who believe in the virgin birth*.

Karl Barth put it as well as it can ever be said once when a student asked him: "Professor, did God reveal himself through any other religion like he did in Christianity?" Barth said gently, "God never revealed himself through any religion. He revealed himself in his son."

Oops!

"To err is human, to forgive is divine"said Alexander Pope, whose wit and wisdom have earned him a seat among the divine. I love his comment on outwitting the moth: "It never made a meal of my best clothes because I wore them every day." Alex was not thinking of sin when he wrote about erring. He knew, I'm sure, that the Apostle wrote *We have all sinned and come short of the glory of God.* Pundits have filled volumes with their views of sin. And what would preachers do if they could not pound the pulpit talk about sin. The congregation might not always understand sin's complexity. One small church member described sins of omission as those sins we should have committed but didn't. And that is all I'm going to say about sin today.

An oops! Is always unintended. Like the one Judge John A. Weeks made in his Minneapolis courtroom. He ordered a man in the back row out of the building for discourteously wearing a hat in the"sacred chambers." When he asked the bailiff to call the next case, that of a Mr. George A. Rogde, the clerk whispered, "Sir, that is the man you ordered out of the court." They're still looking for George.

Now the question is, if you were in that courtroom, would you have laughed, or would you have, like Edith Bunker, stifled it? People laugh at the oops! of others like when someone spills soup on themselves in a restaurant, or when someone's hat blows off and lands in the middle of a lake, or when a prim and proper gentleman slips and falls on the seat of his pants in mud. We could go on. Why is it that we find humor in the discomfort of others? It has been surmised that it is because we, the observers, have been spared a similar fate. Maybe so. I'm not sure.

What I am sure about is that all humor is based on incongruity, the unexpected twist, the surprise ending. To be funny something has to be *incongruous*, which word sounds very much like *in congress* which proves the point, I guess, for much that goes on in those chambers is often sadly funny. Like the father and his son sitting in the balcony of the U.S. Senate. The son asks, "Who is that?"

"That's the chaplain," said the dad, "he opens the session with prayer."

"Does he look at the country and pray for the senators?" asked the boy.

"No," replied the father, "he looks at the senators and prays for the country."

If we slip up on a banana peel we cannot avoid being on the butt end (pun intended) of an oops! And being laughed at. When an embarrassing thing does happen to us, we should just smile, like on Candid Camera, and say, well, I guess this proves I'm human. Or even better, join those who laugh, thus following the Biblical admonition *to laugh with those who laugh and weep with those who weep.* That would be forgiving ourselves and maybe becoming a little more divine?

I hope one student I heard of was able to do this in a botany class. The professor held up a plant and said, "This belongs to the begonia family." This student, trying to make points, said, "Are you keeping it for them while they are away?" She was human. I hope the professor was divine.

Temptation

A little angel on a white cloud, next to God's throne, says, "Maybe it would have been a good thing to put a warning label on that apple." On the face of it the little angel's idea seems good. But after some thinking on our part God's idea doesn't seem so bad. If he had put a sign on Sampson's hair: *DANGER! DO NOT CUT!* we'd never have had that gripping story with the lessons it conveys. And the Bible would have been a weak book without all the lessons we readers learn from seeing the results of wrong choices Bible characters made.

When Eve saw that red Macintosh hanging from the tree in the garden, curiosity took over. She picked one, showed it to Adam and asked, "What is this?" And of course Adam said, "I'll bite," and there started the whole kit and caboodle of failings and transgressions that theologians have been explaining and preachers sermonizing about ever since.

I'm sure when God found out about this first peccadillo he asked Adam to explain. And of course Adam, like men have ever since, said, "It wasn't my fault, God. It was that woman you gave me; she made me do it." But God was not convinced. Later he asked the serpent, "You were there, you must have seen the whole thing; whose fault was it really?" And the serpent said, "Hiss."

I am pondering here the origin of temptation. The word comes from the L. *temptare*, which had the sense of "to feel," "to try out." By extension temptation is related to wonder and curiosity. Now we have to ask, why did God create us with the urge to probe and discover? And the quickest way to the answer is to ask, what if he had not put curiosity into us at the factory?

The answer is that in that case we would be less than brutes, for even the lowest form of mammal is inordinately curious. Put one in a new environment and activity is furious for a while, till the animal has accustomed itself to the new environment. If we had no curiosity there would be no words (why name something if you don't care what it is?) and thus no communication. No communication: no philosophy, religion, science, or love. We can thank God for curiosity which draws out these life-enhancing human behaviors.

But what of the other side of temptation? Not life-enhancing but life-diminishing behaviors? I'm positive that if we asked God why we could not have "good" curiosity only, he would say, "My child, you would never know the meaning of life-enrichment without knowing its opposite, life-impairment." And boy do we know all about life-impairing behavior! The media have made it sickeningly vivid. Even men of the cloth are not immune to temptation. Why should we be? Jesus was tempted. As the Bible tells us: *We do not have a high priest who is unable to sympathize with our weaknesses, but we have one who was tempted in every way just as we are, yet was without sin.*

One older clergyman was asked by a younger one how he dealt with women counselees who flirt. He responded: "Whenever I notice a flirtatious gleam in a counselee's eye, I always check to make sure it isn't a reflection from the gleam in my own."

Don't blame others for tempting us till we're sure we don't *want* to be tempted. Each day our wake-up prayer should include a request for help in facing temptations. Like the little boy who prayed: "And please, God, don't let the ice cream wagon come down our street tomorrow."

His mother said, "Why do you ask that?"

"Because," he said, "I've saved up my allowance and I have just enough to get that baseball bat I've been wanting. But if that truck comes before I get the bat, I'm afraid the ice cream might win.

Like that little boy, we need to keep "prayed up," as preachers said when I was a lad. Martin Luther knew this. When asked how he overcame the Devil, he replied, "Well, when he comes knocking at the door of my heart, the dear Lord Jesus opens it and says, 'Martin Luther used to live here but he moved out.' The Devil sees the nail prints in the hands, turns white and beats a hasty retreat."

Maybe Adam and Eve didn't say their wake-up prayers that day.

Symbols of Faith

I remember the time I got a "C" on my report card. My father was upset so I said, "It's only a symbol," and he replied, "Yes, and I know what the symbol means." He then proceeded to outline some symbol changing behavior on my part.

The dictionary defines *symbol* as "that which indicates the existence of something else." Words are symbols. They stand for something else—they have meaning. The word *dictionary* is not the dictionary itself. Even the word *God*, no matter how reverently it is uttered, is a symbol. Many kinds of body language are symbolic, too: a smile, a wave, a frown, even a tear. Each is what it is but also stands for something else. Thus praying, saying the statement of faith or even preaching are symbolic events. If we fold our hands or kneel we are using body language symbolically. Religion and faith would be poor indeed without symbols.

Symbol means "matching together," and comes from the ancient custom of fitting broken ends of a stick together for verification. One half of the stick was meaningless by itself, but put together—*sym*—the two halves became one and had meaning. For instance, a knight rides up to a castle and says to the Baron, "I come from Sir John. I have this stick. He said you would send him aid." The baron takes out his stick, they fit them together and they match, so the aid is sent on its way to Sir John. Meaning was created. The stick became a symbol.

Religion by its nature must be symbolic because we cannot apprehend God directly. Our end of the stick (our symbols) the cross, candles, flowers, the steeple, the open Bible, the altar, etc. are held out with the hope and faith that they will fit and become reality for us. God held out his end of the stick when his Son was broken on the cross. Worship is holding our brokenness (our end of the stick) up to God—seeking a match and wholeness.

We do the same thing when we enter into the rite of communion. We are seeking for wholeness, a match for our brokenness. I was sixteen when I was baptized in the Potomac River outside of Washington, D.C. It was a chilly day and I shivered, coming out of the water, but my heart was warm as I joined the others on the riverbank in songs and prayers.

Tom Wallace, former pastor of a Baptist church in Elkton, MD., wrote about one convert who had no religious upbringing but who was ecstatic with his new-found faith. When he came out of the baptistry in the church he raised his hands and, instead of alleluia he shouted, "Hot dog! Hot dog! Hot dog!" The congregation began to titter but Tom hushed them with the admonition: "God hears the spirit of the words as well as the words themselves," reminiscent of Paul's answer to the Romans about prayer: *He who searches our hearts knows the mind of the spirit.*

In the first century it was dangerous for an early Christian to speak about Jesus openly, so a symbol of recognition was devised. It was the picture of a fish. A Christian, believing another person near him was also Christian, would draw a fish in the dirt. If he was correct, the other person would begin sharing his faith. A fish in front of a house would convey the same information about that household

It was not by chance that "fish" was chosen as the symbol. The Greek word for fish in the N.T. is *ichthyos* (from which comes the word "ichthyology" meaning the study of fish.) Each Greek letter was a symbol which when put together meant Jesus Christ, Son of God, Savior. The sign of the fish was frequently used on the crypts in which the early Christians were buried.

Symbols can be very powerful. The church that informed my developing years used the symbolic "laying on of hands" and annointing with oil. Ministers followed the Biblical injunction *Is any one of you sick? He should call the elders of the church to pray over him and anoint him with oil in the name of the Lord.* The ministers I knew did this. None of them, I'm sure, believed the power lay in the olive oil itself. If that were true the stock in olive oil companies would go out of sight. The power was in the sign used *in the name of the Lord.* Because of her belief my grandmother was made to see again after being blind for two years.

Christ is God holding toward us his end of the broken stick. Our fractured lives will always match if we let go and let God—that is if we don't try too hard to force the fit. And when this happens miracles occur.

Maybe even if it's only the miracle of an A we get in school.

That's Right Up My Alley . . .

. . . could mean *I have a talent for that* which by extension means some people don't have a talent for that. We are each a bundle of differing talents. I don't have a talent for singing. I'm just not cut out for it. I'm like the gingerbread man who looked at a chocolate bit, Oreo and ginger snap and said sadly, "I'm just not cut out to be a cookie."

Are we, like the gingerbread man, "cut out to be" a particular thing? Or can we be anything we choose if we are willing to put enough time and effort into it? You'll find people in both camps, but ask yourself honestly, could a man five feet tall make the Celtics basketball team? Or could a five-foot-tall beauty become Miss America? From a more staid and practical sense, could one of us be a Mozart if we spent enough time at the piano?

Let's agree: there are things right down our alley besides a bowling ball. There is such a thing as talent. People do have "bents" or "leanings" toward one ability or another. Born that way. We are not clones, not cut with the same pattern. In some ways we are like all other people, but in other ways we are like no other person. How happy we should be that God did not make us all exactly alike. I've often said that if we were all exactly alike, every man would want Polly for his wife.

This is good news and bad news. The good news is freedom of choice. We don't have to be gingerbread men cut by a mold not of our choosing. The bad news is responsibility—the obligation to become all that we can be. Or is it an obligation? Jesus' parable makes me think so. When the man with one talent buried it instead of developing it Jesus was brutally frank. *Take therefore the talent from him . . . and cast the unprofitable servant into outer darkness.* We each have a responsibility to discover, express and develop our differences. A healthy family, church or nation demands this. God didn't force us into a mold. He gave us the thrilling task of finding out and developing *to the best of our ability* what we can be. He put the burden and the glory on our shoulders. It is not so thrilling, though when the task is more burden than glory.

I was the pastor of a young woman in Bradford who sang in the choir, was a member of women's groups and was Johnny on the spot when there was cleaning to be done around the church. But she was mentally challenged. She supported herself doing housework. She came to my study for counseling. She said, "Why don't boys ask me for a date? I want to get married some day, like other girls, and have children of my own."

Dear reader, I can't describe my anguish at that point. I was tongue-tied. My heart was bleeding. How do you explain to one of God's children that she can't be all that she wants to be for him? How do you explain that God loves her more than most of his other children? Would she understand why? I don't remember how the counseling session ended, but I know I thanked her and praised her for her work in God's church. In my eyes she was the man with one talent, except she didn't bury it but worked at it for all she was worth.

Like a patient in a mental hospital who wanted desperately to get out. He asked his doctor what he could do to prove he was ready. The doctor gave him a textbook on anatomy and told him to come back when he had mastered it. The patient came back in about a month and announced he was ready. "Point to and name the different parts of your arm," said the doctor. The patient successfully identified the hand, the wrist, the forearm, etc. and was given his release. while walking out, papers in hand, another patient said to him admiringly, "How did you do it?" The first patient pointed to his right temple and said, "Kidneys, man, kidneys." We each have our talents and none are too small to be used by God.

Sir Michael Costa, the celebrated conductor, was holding a rehearsal. As the mighty chorus rang out, accompanied by hundreds of instruments, the piccolo player ceased playing, thinking his small part would not be missed among so many. Suddenly the great conductor stopped and cried out, "Where is the piccolo?" The sound of that one small instrument was necessary to the harmony.

The young lady mentioned above was one of God's piccolos. She is a necessary part in God's celestial orchestra. In my opinion, excuses about our "piccolo size" won't carry much weight with Jesus. He isn't going to say, "Considering the kind of parents you had and the neighborhood you grew up in, I don't blame you for burying your talent." On the other hand I can see him saying to a scrub woman who put her kids through college "Come, sit at my right hand and tell me the exciting story of how you made it through those tough years." And the girl from Bradford will be there and so will my sainted grandmother who only went to the third grade. They will be surprised at how many like them there are and how eager the angels are to hear their tales.

The Good Old Days

A man was chiding his son for the poor grades he got in history. "Why, when I was your age, I thought history was easy!"

"Easy for you!" the son exclaimed. "Those were your good old days—you were living then."

What does that mean, ***good old days?*** Does it mean all "old" days are good? Or that all "good" days are in the past?

Neither of these, of course. The phrase *good old days* is the outer sign of an inner activity called nostalgia, from the Greek *nostos* (return home) plus *algia* (pain)—*a painful desire to go back home.* We're still left with the question, "Why do we get nostalgic?" Why do we hear the phrase *the good old days* so often?

Could it be the desire for safety and comfort?

Could be. Take a newborn. It emerges from the womb, is held up by the heels, given a spank to start breathing, a stylus rubbed across the soles of its feet and the palms of its hands to check nerve reactions, its throat is swabbed out, drops put in its eyes, dried off with a rough towel and it yells. The meaning of that yell is probably, "Put me back in there! It's too rough and dangerous out here! I want the good old days!"

Nostalgia is built into us at the factory. It's automatic. It's like grammar: past perfect, present tense, future conditional. Let's look at that last word *conditional.* It means the outcome of something is not certain. Uncertainty is a two-edged sword. We can't live with it and we can't live without it.

There would be no such thing as games and sports if the outcome of everything were certain. How dull to hear the coach say, "OK, now, I know it's not exciting to play a game in which we have to be losers fifteen to three, but that's the way it is. We have to look involved, anyway. The fans expect it of us. The next game on the docket we win by twenty-three to one." And many people seek certain types of employment because they like the challenge, the uncertainty in it.

Looking back, things were more certain in the old days. You could grease the wheels on the buggy and feed oats to the horse, and your transportation problems were solved.

And even if you fell asleep at the reins, you knew what to expect—the horse knew the way and would take you home. This happened to my grandfather. On the way home from work he would fall asleep in the buggy and not wake up till the horse stopped at the farmhouse door. But then modernization reared its ugly head, and Grandpa, to keep up with the times, bought a Model T Ford. One day driving home he fell asleep at the wheel and the car did not know the way home. He ended up in the hospital and died soon after.

At that point my grandmother would be wishing most fervently for the good old days.

And things were also simpler in the good old days. You didn't need a plumber if the three-holer got clogged. You dug a new hole and moved the outhouse. Simple. And don't we still fall back on the kerosene lamp now and then when the electricity fails us? But is that the basis for the nostalgia about the good old days? The simplicity of it all?

No, not for me, or most of us, or at least not most of the time. Rather, I believe, nostalgia increases in direct proportion to the increase in the complexity of life. We long for simplicity. Things were quite simple back in the Garden of Eden, though one could even then get kicked out for breaking the condo rules. And as history progressed the Bible gives us pictures of ever more complex situations till God had to hand down a rule book to help humans master the complexities of living.

Is there no end to the expanding convolutions of life? There are many who feel that we are being overwhelmed with complexity. One of the most respected futurists, Alvin Toffler, in his book *Future Shock,* predicted back in 1970 "I don't believe that the system can continue in its present form." Looking down at us from up there, Alvin, what do you think?

I think what God said to Isaiah three thousand years ago is as true for us as it was for him: *This is what the LORD says, Fear not, for I have redeemed you; I have summoned you by name; you are mine. When you pass through the waters, I will be with you; and when you pass through the rivers, they will not sweep over you. When you walk through the fire, you will not be burned and the flames will not set you ablaze.*

No matter what the confusion, the uncertainty or complexity of our lives, we are always in the "good old days" with God.

A Place of One's Own

While going through some papers in my family tree file, I came across a 70-year-old obituary from the Pelston, Michigan News. It is the obit of my grandmother, Elizabeth Bowden Hicks. The brown with age article said: "Mrs. Hicks died at her home in Pelston at age 82. She was married at age 14 and had 10 children (their names followed), 18 grandchildren (their names followed) and 30 great-grandchildren." I was one of the 30 great-grandchildren, unnamed in the obituary. Not much of an ego booster.

The last time we traveled north from Kalamazoo to Pelston to see Gramma Hicks I was four years old, perhaps five. I remember a small clapboard house, unpainted, with a covered porch on which there was a glider swing. I thought that was neat. We didn't have one of those. In my mind's eye I still see Gramma sitting by her kitchen table on which lay a Bible. She was in a rocker and smoking a white clay pipe. I'm sure some of the "saints" did a tsk-tsk about that, but for one who spent her years raising ten children and taking care of a lumberjack husband, and knowing her Bible cover-to-cover, it could be allowed. She knew that her Lord had said, *In my father's house are many rooms. I go to prepare a place for you*. She labored long and hard to establish a place for her and her family on earth, and I believe she, in her white rocker, was simply waiting to be transported to the place prepared for her in God's house. I'm sure that when God called her to the room he had prepared for her, he said, "There'll be an ashtray on the table."

Her place in life wasn't much by today's standards, but it was her place. And knowing that she had a place in glory, the place on earth was not as important as it otherwise might have been. There was no TV, radio, shelf of books, running water, or even a white porcelain sanitary facility, but it was her place. What there was, however, in the rude house in which she, her husband Artemus and their ever growing family lived, was games, singing, work, chores, and a bearskin rug which Mary, one of the ten, provided.

Mary had gone out to bring in some wood for the stove, and accidentally got in between a she-bear and her cubs. She picked up an armful of wood and started back to the house, only to be faced with the she bear, reared and coming toward her. Aunt Mary dropped the wood and grabbed the axe to fight for her life, a brave but pointless endeavor had it not been for the family dog that had followed her out. The dog bit at the bear's heels and when the bear turned to swipe at the dog, Mary swung the axe. When the bear turned toward her, the dog bit at it's heels, and this went on till the bear lay bloody and dead. The bear "lived on" in the form of a rug on the living room floor. I saw it when we traveled north to see Gramma Hicks. You don't get excitement like that these days. It all went to make it a place of their own.

The need for this "sense of place" can be seen wherever we look. Children fight for it at the table and in the family car; some mental hospitals have only rectangle shaped tables on the wards instead of round because it is easier for a patient to identify his place at the table; pictures on one's desk at work; owners picking through the ashes of a home that was burned, looking for something to put in their next home to carry on that sense of place. And as we know, the place of one's own extends even to the church.

Doctor Garland was the head usher in the Bradford, Massachusetts church I served. He was one of the best. When his wife, Alice, died something about his *place* was twisted and askew, as it is with all of us when a piece of our life is cut away and we hobble about, spiritually crippled, for a while. But he, like the rest, did little things to keep the *place* as meaningful as possible. For instance, every Sunday morning Dr. Garland took a bulletin and placed it in the hymnal rack in front of the pew seat that had, for a lot of years, been Alice's place. If anyone inadvertently sat there he would say to the person, "That's Alice's place; please sit somewhere else." Dr. Garland was a bit less lonely when Alice's bulletin was in place and her seat ready.

A Peanuts cartoon has little Linus afraid to be alone in the library. Charlie Brown tries to explain to him that everyone is lonely in some place or other. "Where is that place for you?" Linus asks. Charlie ponders the question for a moment, then answers: "Earth."

That's sad. It reminds me of people huddled in refugee camps, waiting to be allowed to cross a border and begin establishing a place of their own again. We hear the phrase, "they have only what's on their back," and the tragic reality of it is hard for us to grasp, we who have such a plethora of things to identify our place.

Utter loneliness accompanies the loss of sense of place, a sense of no place of our own. It is a painful condition, a situation of which God must have been aware when he created us. A Frank and Ernest cartoon has an angel saying to God, "I think the man you created is suffering from loneliness," and God replies, "Yes, I've been thinking of splitting the Adam."

He did and gave them a place of their own, Eden. But he had to cancel the lease and cast them out of Eden when they disobeyed him. He cast them out but he did not abandon them. He still walked with them and talked with them. Even though they had been naughty, they were still his own.

Gramma Hicks knew what it was to walk and talk with God. It was probably the largest piece of her sense of place. And it should be so for you and me.

If you want to get further confirmation, Call Eve and ask her, yourself. Her number is Adam 812.

In Memory of the Boll Weevil

Polly and I were traveling in Alabama a few years ago and I looked up a town I had heard of called Enterprise. In the town square I found the monument I was looking for. The plaque on it read

> *This monument is erected*
> *in thankful memory*
> *to the cotton boll weevil.*

It then went on to explain how, many years ago, the boll weevil had destroyed the town's cotton crop three years in a row. The town was devastated. The people got together to decide what to do. There were a few votes to leave, thus creating a ghost town, but most of them agreed to work together to overcome the difficulty. They decided to diversify. Today Enterprise exists as a much wealthier town than it ever could have been as a cotton town. And all because of a little worm which seemed to have them on the ropes years ago. Its citizens are thankful for ancestors who had the courage to change, to dare and to risk.

The word *thank* is from the same root as the word *think* Thus a person who takes a gift or favor from someone and doesn't thank him is thoughtless. He doesn't think about his own good fortune or and about the kindness of the giver. He's thinkless. In a thankless heart the very fires of life have turned to ashes.

In the last century a family was spending the summer at a lake resort. The son, Sandy, was playing on a wharf when he fell in the water. He would have drowned except for the efforts of a man who pulled him out and gave him artificial respiration. When Sandy came to, he saw the stranger looking down at him and realized the situation. He said, "Thank you, mister for saving my life."

All the man said was, "Just make sure you are worth saving."

Many years later Bishop Bruce Baxter would speak to a hushed congregation when he told this story, for he ended it with, "That little boy was me. Hardly a day has gone by that I have not felt deep gratitude in my heart for that man's caring and bravery."

I wonder about us. Are we grateful for the privilege of just being alive, of just being able to appreciate friends, flowers, food, and the thousand other daily gifts we so easily forget?

Consider the fourth grader who listed his glasses as something he thanked God for. When his Sunday School teacher asked him to explain he said, "Because they keep the big boys from punching me and the girls from kissing me."

Or think of the parishioner who was forced into bankruptcy. His pastor said, "There's always something to be thankful for."

"Name one," said the man. "That you aren't one of your creditors," said the minister.

Thanksgiving is a time to resolve to be more aware of the countless blessings that permeate our lives and to lift a grateful heart to God. And if we can't think of anything else, let us be grateful that we are not the bird that will be on our table this Thanksgiving.

God In Our Playpen

A grandfather was keeping an eye on his grandchild who was in a playpen. Whoever coined that name *playpen* wasn't thinking. A pen doesn't seem conducive to playing. I suppose pigs play in the pigpen and maybe convicts play solitaire in the state pen, but the very word *pen* has the sense of confinement and comes from the same root as *pent*. And so it was this day for the grandchild. She was pent up. She wanted freedom. She wanted to be picked up and lifted out of the pen, so her arms were held toward grandfather and little noises were heard by him as "get me out of here." He wanted nothing more than to oblige so He arose, went to the playpen and reached in, ready to rescue his grandchild. But just then the child's mother entered the room, took one look at what was going on and said, "Put that child down! She must learn that she cannot always get her way by fussing and holding up her arms. She's perfectly alright in there. It's good discipline." So, sadly, Grandfather put the child back in the pen.

But then Grandpa got an idea. In astonishment the mother saw grandpa lift one leg and put it in the playpen then lift the other to do the same, after which he sat down in the playpen with his grandchild and began to play.

In my sixty years of preaching, this story illuminates most clearly the deep meaning of *Immanuel—God with us*. Whenever I hear, read or sing *Immanuel* I see this picture of God placing one leg, then the other, then his whole self into my pen. Whatever my confinement, he is there with me. We all have many kinds of bars around us. We are alone. We are hurting. We are depressed. We have so many needs. we need forgiveness. Yet all we have to do is become aware that God in Jesus climbed into our playpen a long time ago.

In another land in another time a prisoner sat on the dirt floor, pulled his cloak a little tighter around him and shared his bread with a rat that scampered across the floor. Then through the bars of the one small window he heard people singing: "O come, all ye faithful, joyful and triumphant." And he knew. It was Christmas eve. With all his heart he wanted to obey the words of that song—to come with all the worshipers to the church on the hill—but he could not. In his mind he could see the people marching up with their candles. At midnight he knew the mass was being celebrated and he went over in his mind what he could remember of it. The kind of life he had led made him avoid the church. He heard the bells ring. He strained to hear what he could of the music. He knelt and in his way participated in the mass. Then he heard the bells and knew it was midnight. Christmas day had come. He prayed and as he prayed tears ran down his cheeks. "Forgive me, for I have sinned. I am not worthy to be in your cathedral." Then he heard a voice as plain as ever man spoke saying, "Rise my son. Your sins are forgiven. You are worthy to be with me in my kingdom." There was a dim presence—a luminous white figure. "Master," the prisoner said, "I wanted so to be with you in the Cathedral!"

"Don't you know, my son," said Jesus, "I am up there on the hill once a year, but I am down here every day." *Arise, shine, for your light has come. He tends his flock like a shepherd. He gathers the lambs in his arms and carries them close to his heart. Do you not know? Have you not heard? The Lord, God gives strength to the weary and increases the power of the weak.*

God is in our playpen with us.

Oval Souls and Iron Beds

A young girl had been seeing the school psychologist because her behavior didn't seem to fit in with that of her classmates. After several sessions she wrote her doctor a letter. "Dear doctor Matthews: I never know what to say when we are talking so I thought I would write you this letter. I know I am different and I think I know why, but it is difficult to explain. You see, we live on a round planet, but not all planets are round. Some are oval, some are square, some are even like a triangle. God made them that way. When he makes people he puts a soul in their body the shape of the planet they are going to live on. My problem is that he put an oval soul in me and then made the mistake of putting me on a round planet. All my life my parents and school teachers, and even you, Doctor Matthews, have been pushing and scraping on my soul to make it round like everyone else's, and all I want is to be left alone with my oval soul. Love, Susie."

One of life's big problems, from childhood on, is to fit in—fit in with family members, with playmates, with children at school, and lastly, with society. And Susie was right. Grownups were squeezing, filing and shaping her soul into the normal shape. Susie, however was willing and eager to stay as she was—different—oval. I'm still of two minds about this. I read about people who have made great contributions to society by being different and I think, "We should protect and foster the differences." Then I see tragic situations. At least they seem tragic to me. Like the following.

While I was pastor in Abington, Massachusetts, there was a hermit living in town. He lived apart from other people in a small house he constructed. He did odd jobs to earn enough to support himself, and as far as I knew was satisfied with his oval soul. He began attending our church and of course, because of his clothes, stood out like a sore thumb. Few people talked with him, but that didn't seem to bother him. A crisis arose when he asked me if he could join the choir. I told him to see the choir director. He did and the choir director auditioned him and had to accept him because he had a fine tenor voice. Things were OK for about a month but then the choir—with good intentions, I'm sure—presented him with a new suit, shirt, tie and shoes. He stopped coming to church.

To the iron beds.

The ancient myths speak to the fundamental verities of life. Procrustes lived by the side of the road and invited travelers to stop for a good meal and a night's rest. He had an iron bed they were to sleep on, but if they were too long for it, he chopped off their legs to fit. If they were too short, he put them on the rack and stretched them to fit.

We had a great choir in Abington, but even good choirs have their little iron beds one has to fit if they are to become an accepted member.

I have no pedestal to stand on. I have done my share of squeezing a soul here and there into what I thought would be a more pleasing shape. And I have, on occasion, put an acquaintance on my iron bed, thinking they would be better off a bit shorter or a bit taller. I haven't cut off any legs, but I can't say I haven't wanted to.

All parents know about this because it is their legitimate task to prepare their children for the trials and tribulations of the culture they are in. Perhaps if they squeeze a bit too hard on a soul now and then, they can be forgiven. One mother was angry because her little one kept raiding the cookie jar. One day he said to her, "The temptation is just too great, Mom."

His mother answered, "The next time the devil tempts you to raid the cookie jar, say, "Get thee behind me, Satan!"

Of course it happened again and when taken to task, the little one said, "I told old Satan to get behind me and he did—but he pushed me right into the cookie jar!"

Perhaps Mom should shorten Satan's legs a bit.

Defining Moments . . .

. . . are those in which the meaning or purpose of something becomes startlingly clear, often with a life-changing result. Take Helen Keller's experience for example.

Blind and deaf due to a life-threatening fever in early childhood, Helen grew up in a dark and silent world. She communicated somewhat with her parents through noises and charade-like gestures. Then Anne Sullivan came into her life as a private tutor. With her finger she taught Helen the alphabet by spelling out letters in the palm of her hand. Helen enjoyed the game but the letters meant nothing to her—they didn't *define* anything. Then Anne got the idea of making a connection between the game of letters and the real world. She held Helen's hand under the water from a pump and immediately after spelled out in her hand the letters W-A-T-E-R. It took some time, but after one of those lessons Helen froze. She realized that the letters spelled out in her hand defined the cold, wet stuff coming from the pump. She rushed about touching everything she could find and holding out her hand to have Anne spell it out to her. *A defining moment.*

I met Helen Keller when she was sixty-two years old and I was twenty-seven. I was a hospital corpsman in the Naval Hospital in Portsmouth, NH. Helen was "visiting the troops." We lined up and she went to each one of us, making conversation. She came to me, held my face in her hands with her thumbs on my lips and her palms under my chin. Her sightless eyes looked into mine and she said, "What is your favorite book?"

"The Bible," I said.

With her hands as her ears, feeling the vibrations in my lips and throat, she said, "Mine, too." At that moment I sensed a truth too big for words. *Our creative spirits can be mightier than the obstacles which try to block them.* A defining moment of my own.

One of the truly great defining moments of Christendom occurred on the road to Damascus when the Apostle Paul nearly died from an attack of his recurrent physical ailment, *an affliction given me, a thorn in my flesh, a messenger of Satan, to torment me. Three times I pleaded with the Lord to take it away from me. But he said to me, "My grace is sufficient for you, for my power is made perfect in weakness."* Paul was struck blind then saw a great light. He experienced the presence of Christ and there burst upon his consciousness a new, life-encompassing definition of reality that demanded a new loyalty. Paul was converted to the very Christianity he had been trying to destroy—a defining moment par excellence! It not only changed him but it changed the world.

I was fortunate to share in one man's defining moment. He, along with his daughter and his wife, was a member of my Death and Dying Class at Northern Essex College. He knew he was dying and had come with his family to learn to face the reality with courage and hope. I got a telephone call that he had a relapse and was in the hospital. They thought he had died, but he came back—a near death experience. At the next class we all jumped in our cars, went to the Hale Hospital and spent the whole two hours at his bedside. He described the light he encountered and the voice he "heard" that seemed to say "love," not the word but the understanding. "Now," he said, "I love everything. I have never felt so much love! I love every one of you. I love the bird that lands on the window sill. I love the nurse that brings my medicine, I even love the boy who cleans my room with his mop. It was obvious that this had been a defining moment for him. I know it was for the class.

He had what at the time was called an "out of body experience." I recall a Frank and Ernest cartoon. Frank and Ernest are two huge shapeless individuals. Ernest says to Frank, "I had an Out of the Body Experience." Frank looked at his formless body and said, "I don't blame you."

Besides out of the body experiences which occur near death there are scientific breakthroughs when a new understanding floods the mind. One of the most famous of these happened to Archimedes, the greatest mathematician and engineer of Ancient times. He was a Greek from Syracuse, who was killed when the city was besieged by the Romans in 212 B.C. His fame is linked to the "Archimedes' principle." It seems that the king had a problem. People gave him articles presumably made of gold. But was it really gold? He gave the problem to Archimedes who thought and figured but could come up with nothing till one day while taking a bath. When he got in the tub he noticed the level of the water rising. The story goes that he jumped from the tub and ran down the street naked shouting, "Eureka! Eureka," which means "I have found it!" He had discovered the principle of displacement. Everything, when immersed in water, will displace a specific amount of the liquid. Put gold in a container of water and it will displace a given amount of liquid. Put another metal in the water, etc. If the gold was an alloy, it would not displace the same amount of water as pure gold. An historic defining moment had occurred.

Could the moral of this be—we should take baths not showers—and think while doing it? Maybe we would learn something and become wiser. Solomon was pretty wise and he wrote to us in Proverbs *Let the wise listen and add to their learning*. He probably thought of this while taking a bath. They didn't have showers in his day, and besides, it is hard to hear yourself think with the shower running.

But You Don't Understand

A man rushed to a farmer's house and said, "Please come down to the swamp and help me pull my boy out of the mud!"

"How deep is he in?" asked the farmer.

"Up to his ankles," replied the father.

"OK, I'll come down, but we've got lots of time. Come in for a cup of coffee."

"But you don't understand!" yelled the father. "He's in upside down."

Understand is the operative word here. I'm not going to waste time figuring out how the kid got in the mud upside down, but the situation illuminates the meaning of a *lack of understanding.* The Bible gets right to the hub of the matter when it says *Wisdom is supreme; therefore get wisdom. Though it costs all you have get understanding.* Wisdom and understanding are not interchangeable. Understanding is in your thinking. Wisdom is in your doing.

Like the woman who was trying on a dress. She asks her husband his opinion about the dress. He likes the dress but how he tells her makes a big difference. He might say, "That dress makes you look beautiful," or he might say, "You make that dress look beautiful." If you know which answer is the wiser one, you are well on your way to getting understanding.

Every great culture had its wise men and their collections of wise sayings. Solomon, king of Israel some nine hundred years before Christ, is credited with the authorship of the Book of Proverbs or wise sayings, like *Go to the ant, you sluggard; consider its ways and be wise! It has no commander, no overseer or ruler, yet it stores its provisions in summer and gathers its food at harvest.*

Another such collection of wisdom was that of Ptahhotep, a wise man living in Egypt a thousand years before Solomon. One of his many recommendations reads *If you dispute with a man while he is angry, do not look down on him because he is angry but you are not; do not toy with his feelings. It is the act of a despicable soul so to do. If you begin to get angry, combat this desire as a thing unacceptable to all great men.*

Such sayings are intuitively correct and true. They are wise. On hearing them a light goes on in your brain. I remember such an occurrence in my sophomore year of college. My psychology teacher said, "Remember, when you are in an argument and you are beginning to get angry, you have already lost." Of all the things I learned in that class, that's the only one I remember. Wise sayings stick with us.

Back to Solomon. He says *Wisdom is supreme, therefore get wisdom.* How does one GET it? Out of a book? In school—Wisdom 101? At the feet of a guru? We know how Solomon got wisdom. He prayed for it. *Give me wisdom that I may lead this people, for who is able to govern your great people?* And God answered *Since you have not asked for wealth, riches or honor, nor for the death of your enemies, and since you have not asked for long life but for wisdom to govern your people, wisdom will be given you. And I will give you riches and honor such as no king before you had.*

The wisest thing to do is ask God in prayer and go on from there. Gee I created a proverb. Not really. God gave it to me.

So we pray to God for wisdom and then study what the wise men say. One of the wise sayings of the author of Ecclesiastes is *The more the words the less the meaning.*

I'm wise enough to take a hint.

Diets Are For . . .

. . . . people who are thick and tired of it.

But not just those. There's at least one other use for the word *diet*. The word springs from the Greek *diaeta* which comes from "day," or a days worth of something: a day's work, a day's food, a day's travel. From "day's work" came the name of a legislative body called the diet. This is still the name of some national legislative bodies, as in Japan. In the middle ages this was the name of church councils which met to decide on thorny issues. Thus it was that my church history professor, Dr. Edwin Prince Booth would say, with a twinkle in his eye, "Nothing so upset the digestion of the Catholic Church as the Diet of Worms."

The Diet of Worms (a city in Germany) was the trial for heresy of Martin Luther in 1521. He was asked to recant his negative statements about the church or be excommunicated. He stood his ground, summing up his testimony with the famous proclamation *Here I stand. I cannot do otherwise. God help me. Amen.*

And so was born the Reformation and Protestantism. A church on a diet?

We, however, when we think of diet, think of food, delicious food. With apologies to the great bard *what foods these morsels be!* We blame the food we eat for many of our ills, giving rise to the American public's love affair with diet plans, half believing they could be the answer to all their ills. Not common sense, not will power, but just the right diet plan.

A bit of research of the Internet reveals there to be over 1200 diet books available. I was intrigued by some of their titles. For instance *The Afterlife Diet*, by Daniel Pinkwater. I assume it has to do with milk and honey—and perhaps some manna to spread the honey on.

Then there is the book *God's Diet* by Gault McNamee. I can't begin to guess what that is about, but certainly, if it is good enough for God, it's good enough for me.

The Creationist Diet by Gary Zeola just has to be based on apples. But to get serious.

There are people who for one reason or another must be on rigid diets; their lives depend on it. And not because of any life mismanagement on their part. My niece, Becky, for instance, was allergic to wheat. Imagine the task of planning a diet without any wheat in it. Not even any Breakfast of Champions! And there's the diabetic diet, the low cholesterol diet, and many others.

Diet played a striking part in the emergence of God's Chosen People. The kosher diet became so central to Jewish religion that to violate the kosher laws was to violate God. *Break these laws and you will be vomited out* it says in Leviticus.

Thus it was that when Daniel was a slave in a foreign land and a servant of the king, he refused to eat the food that came from the king's table. It wasn't kosher. He was lucky that one of the king's stewards agreed on a trial diet. He asked that he and his friends be given a vegetarian diet for ten days. The outcome was a great success and Daniel and friends were in better physical condition than the natives. Just goes to show that vegetables and water are better for our health than Twinkies and Coke, or as the Bible says the King's table was laden with "rich food." In other words Nebuchadrezzar partook of an unbalanced diet.

One man achieved a balanced diet by putting his meat and vegetables on one side of a balance scale and his dessert on the other side. The dessert side was up in the air, so he kept putting more sweets on till it was even with the fruits and vegetables.

For our spiritual health the best diet is bread and water. Jesus called himself the bread of life and the water of life. Keep reading his words—the bread—and through prayer stay in tune with his spirit—the water of life—and you will be strong in your soul. This has been my life's aim.

For my stomach, though, I still would like to know more about that Methuselah diet.

To Sleep: Perchance to Dream . . .

Have you ever fallen asleep in church? I have, and I think I'm one of an army of church sleepers. I don't know whether anyone has done a survey of church sleepers, but one analyst reported that "If all the people who fall asleep in church were placed end to end, they would be more comfortable."

Believe it or not, keeping people awake was once a test I had to undergo to see whether I would become the pastor of the church in Bradford, Massachusetts. It was my trial sermon. A member of the church, Dick Anthony, fell asleep in every Sunday service without fail. My task—unbeknownst to me—was to keep him awake.

Well, I did and I served that church for quite a few years, and that man was one of the finest laymen I have known. I recommend that you preachers out there find a person who habitually sleeps during the service and then make it a point to devise the kind of sermons that will keep him or her awake. Such sermons will probably be more interesting to the rest of the congregation. Of course we can't do much about those few preachers who are themselves somniloquists.

One minister I heard of got exasperated with a member who habitually fell asleep during his sermon. The next time he was preaching and the man nodded off, he said, "Everyone who wants to go to Heaven stand up." Of course all stood but this lone sleeper. He then said, "Everyone who wants to go to Hell STAND UP!!" The sleeper awoke and jumped to his feet, looked around and said, "I don't know what we're voting for pastor, but looks like you and I are the only ones for it."

As you can see, we clergy must be careful how we go about trying to keep you lay persons awake. Here's an example of how not to go about this task. It cost one minister his job. Two preachers were sharing the joys and woes of their calling when the topic of sleeping in church came up. Preacher A said, "It gets discouraging. Last Sunday I noticed six people nodding off. I don't know what to do." Preacher B replied, "I had your problem in the past but I discovered a technique for curing it. I say something shocking and the stirring among the members who are not asleep wakes up the sleepers."

"Can you give me a frinstance?" asked Preacher A, and Preacher B said, "Well, one time, noting that several servants of God were *meditating* with their eyes closed and their chins on their chests, I said in a loud voice, 'LAST NIGHT I WAS IN THE ARMS OF A BEAUTIFUL WOMAN AND SHE WAS NOT MY WIFE' . . . (pause) . . . You never heard such stirring and looking around. This woke up the meditators and I continued, 'She was my mother.' Well, you can imagine, no one fell asleep again that morning. I do things like that." "I think you may have solved my problem," said Preacher A. "Thank you so much!"

The very next Sunday Preacher A noticed a couple of heavy-lidded worshipers and decided to attempt the ploy he had heard of. He shouted, "Last night I was in the arms of a beautiful woman . . . . and she was not my wife." In no time flat everyone was sitting upright and wide-eyed. The problem was that Preacher A not only did not set the world on fire with his preaching; he had a poor memory to boot. He paused, trying to recall the rest of the story and finally blurted out, "For the life of me I can't remember who she was." The last I heard he was pumping gas in Alberquerque. We have to be careful.

But seriously, folks, we must remember that sleep is the gift of God. And so is dreaming. You are all aware—being Bible scholars—how often God came to the saints of old in their sleep. The patriarchs had a great regard for dreams. They remembered them, mulled over them, and asked the great dream interpreters, like Joseph, to explain them. They were absolutely convinced that dreams were a sacred part of the language God used with his children. When I think of Jacob wrestling with God, of Daniel preparing Nebuchadnezzar for the future by interpreting his dreams, of Joseph changing the course of history by revealing the meaning of the Pharaoh's dream, of Joseph, Mary and Jesus going home a safer way because of instructions Joseph received in a dream! And what can we say of Paul, directed so often in his dreams about what to say and where to go? What would the Church have been had he not heard in his dreams, "Do not be afraid. You must preach for me in Rome?"

Perhaps we should be more gentle. And perhaps we should even be encouraged to design worship services conducive to relaxation, sleeping and dreaming. I think the next time I see someone asleep in church while I am preaching, I'll say to him, "Amen, brother sleep on. God may be speaking to you in a dream—and I can't compete with that."

As the Worm Turns

One definition of *worm* is: a malicious computer program that slips into your PC uninvited and carries out nefarious schemes. One such scheme might be to erase this letter I am writing or some other valued item I'm saving on my hard disk, thus causing me to spend time writing it again. Or suppose, on Saturday night, it deleted the sermon I have prepared for Sunday? *Worms* can be pretty upsetting. I'm sorry that outlaw computer programmers gave their antisocial creations the name of worm. I like worms. They are a wonderful demonstration of God's thoughtfulness. It is the worms God created I want to talk about—angleworms, earthworms, planaria, etc.

Earthworms are amazing creatures. Their diet is dirt cheap. They create their tunnel-homes by eating the dirt in front of them, crawling a little, eating more dirt, etc. Their digestive system takes whatever nutrients there are from the dirt. They can't leave the digested dirt in the hole or they would be trapped, so they crawl to the surface and get rid of it the same way you or I would. It is estimated that up to 15 million tons of earth per acre are deposited on the surface each year. These deposits are called castings and are rich in chemicals needed for growing plant life. Also soil needs air and the holes dug by our friends the worms accomplish this. Charles Darwin wrote a book *Humus and the Earthworm* in which he stated that without the uncountable numbers of earthworms in the world, vegetation would cease to exist, and then, of course, so would we. Know what amazes me? That this is all a part of God's plan, worms, trees, birds, clouds, people, etc., etc. That God's plans are so intricate that even our existence depends on a creature as lowly as a worm. I'm glad Noah didn't leave those two worms off the Ark. Come to think of it, worms are hermaphroditic, they don't need a mate to reproduce. So maybe there was only one worm on the ark and it is our good fortune that Noah didn't step on it.

We must stop using the word "worm" in derogatory ways: "You worm, you!" "You're lower than a worm!" "Don't try to worm your way out of it!" I'd be tempted to say that gossips must be related to worms because they love dirt, but then the kind of castings they leave wherever they go don't do anybody any good. A worm, like a prophet, is without honor in its own country, but put him in a laboratory of a prestigious university and he becomes of famous. In that milieu the worm even has a journal devoted exclusively to its tricks and antics. It is called *The Worm Runner's Digest.* The editor of the journal, Professor J. V. McConnell and his students at the University of Michigan, have spent many years working with planaria in the laboratories. One of the experiments he does has to do with "how simple can a life form be and still learn?" To test this he puts several planaria in a tank of water. A high wattage light bulb is suspended over the tank. When the light bulb is turned on and off the worms don't seem to notice. Then an electric circuit is attached to the box in such a way that when the light bulb is turned on an electric current goes through the water. Now when the switch is closed the worms tremble and writhe in a frenzy! Several times each day the light—electric current combination is administered to the worms. The question is: will the worms learn the relationship of the shock to the light? Now for the big test. the light is turned on—NO SHOCK—and guess what! The worms writhe anyway. That simple creature with a minuscule brain and almost invisible circulatory system has learned something. It has learned that there is an association between the light and its misery. There's more. He next wants to know where the learning resides. To test this he takes two worms who have learned about the shock and cuts them in half (worms grow the other half again when this happens). Will the new half know about the shock? He cuts off the new part, puts it in the water and lo and behold it wiggles when the light goes on. So, it is theorized that the learning resides in the protoplasm, the stuff, the worm is made of. If that is so, the next experiment should work. He takes a worm that has learned to writhe to the shock, grinds it up and feeds it to two newcomers, fresh out of the ground, who have never been in the tank. After they have digested the *pate de foie worm,* he puts the new worms in the water and they writhe when the light goes on. As we talk about this in psychology class I suggest to my students that maybe we are missing something in our methods of education. If we would simply grind up the well-educated professors, make a "Nutri-slim" shake to be taken—one for each subject—the cost of education could be lowered and the process of education would be speeded up. Think how much your pastor knows and how long it takes for him to transmit it to you. Hmmm! Nahh, probably wouldn't work and even if it did it would taste terrible. But the next time you look down at the ground and see those holes surrounded by the little clay-like rims of earth, look up again and say, "Thank you God for taking such infinite care of our earth. Help us to take care of it, too."

Blacking Your Own Boots

A friend of Abraham Lincoln saw him blacking his boots. "What! Mr. President, you black your own boots?"

"Yes," Abe replied, "whose do you black?"

Lincoln was the epitome of the humble person. Once when a soldier was condemned to death for desertion, the soldier's mother pled with Abe to spare her son's life. Abe wrote out a note of pardon and said, "Give this to Mr. Stanton. He will take care of it." The mother returned with the note, saying, "Secretary Stanton refused to accept the note. He said you were a fool." Abe replied, "Perhaps I am. I'll take care of the matter personally." And he did.

Blessed are the poor in spirit Jesus said to his countrymen two thousand years ago. What did he mean by "poor?" Perhaps today he would have said *Contented and secure are you if you comprehend your ultimate helplessness and put yourself entirely in God's hands.* And is this not the essence of our faith, even the essence of conversion? Jesus went on to say *For then you are already in the Kingdom.* That's why each beatitude starts with *happy (blessed) are they* . . . . Truly, happiness is inherent in being in the Kingdom—being one of the King's kids.

One of my idols has been Roland Hayes, internationally acclaimed tenor, professor at Boston University, grandson of slaves. He was the same person whether singing before the Queen of England or before relatives in their shanties back home in Georgia.

One time, after finishing a concert in Paris he received a telegram from his agent in Berlin. ADVISE CANCELING ENGAGEMENT IN BERLIN (STOP) ANTI-NEGRO SENTIMENT HERE VERY STRONG (STOP) THERE ARE PLANS TO THROW ROCKS AND DRIVE YOU FROM THE STAGE (STOP) PLEASE ADVISE. His manager advised canceling the concert in Berlin, but Roland said, "If the sentiment is that strong in Berlin, it looks like that is where I am meant to be. We'll go."

He walked out on the stage in Berlin, stared for a moment into the blackness of the auditorium, the stage lights illuminating his black face, then lifting his eyes toward heaven he sang "Swing Low, Sweet Chariot." He followed that with "I'm Only a Pilgrim

Here; Heaven Is My Home." Nothing happened. He sang some German folk songs and some light opera and when he finished there was one of the longest standing ovations ever witnessed in that concert hall. Later the cleaning crew picked up bushels of rocks and vegetables from under the seats. His manager said to him, "How do you account for that?" And Roland replied, "When I lifted my eyes to heaven I prayed, 'God, I am your instrument. Sing to these people through me,' and I guess he did."

Humility might just be the most difficult virtue. Pride and all its subdivisions: self esteem, egotism, self indulgence, self-assurance, etc. are urged on us by parents and culture from the cradle. And most of the time they don't get in the way of producing good things for our fellow humans. But once in a while a weakness appears in out character structure that is disastrous and which can only be overcome through humility. Frank Padellero was a friend of mine. We both taught at the same college. He taught economics and did my taxes each year. His weakness was gambling and the weakness almost cost him his life. Some years before it had cost him his home, his marriage and his job. He owed everyone he could possibly squeeze a bit of money out of. Once when his life was threatened unless he paid a forty thousand dollar gambling debt, he got it in bits and pieces and was on his way to pay up when the craving hit again and he went to the track instead. Subsequently he was taken to the Mystic River bridge and hung by his heels. "Forty-eight hours to pay up or you'll be down there," they said. He found Gamblers' Anonymous whose prescription for salvation was give up your self totally and completely to a higher power. He was so sick of the pain and suffering his weakness had caused that he was able to do this. I didn't know him in his earlier days but he was one of the sweetest men I have ever known.

One day his children were staying with him for the weekend. He walked to the corner store for some groceries. On his way back he noticed a crowd in front of his house. As he got close he saw his son's bicycle lying twisted and bent in the street and the driver of a truck bending over it. He dropped his groceries ran to his son, saw that he was all right, set him down saying, "I'll be right back." He rushed into the house, up stairs to his bedroom, knelt at the bed and prayed a prayer of thanksgiving for his son's life and also a prayer of forgiveness for the truck driver. When he came down a neighbor, thinking he had gone in to get a gun, said, "What are you going to do to him Frank?" And Frank said, "I just did it."

The only way to be in the kingdom is being held in the arms of God, and to be held by him we have to be very small.

To Be Or Not To Be

When I Was eighteen a visiting clergyman stayed at our house overnight. He had the other bed in my room. We were both still awake that night when I confided my most momentous decision to him: "Brother Potter," I said (everybody was brother or sister in the church of my youth) "I've decided to give rny life to God as a preacher." He was silent. I was disappointed. I thought he'd be thrilled to see a new soldier entering God's army. After a minute which seemed like eternity he said, "Duane, if there is anything else you can possibly be in this life, be it."

I was nonplused to say the least, but I was then, as I am now, an incurable optimist. I did not take his advice. Fifty-some years later I understand where he was coming from. Ministers are just as subject to trials, tribulations and tears as any layperson. Yet I have always felt lifted up to hear a young person say, "I'm going to be a minister," for in spite of the negative aspects, we also have our share of the three Bs, boons, benefits and blessings.

A few nights ago I heard a 36-year-old man say very similar words: "I'm going to become a priest." I didn't actually hear him say that—I read his message on the Internet which allows us to do fantastic things like talk with people all around the globe. This man, Mac, is a sailor who has two years left on his hitch. Then he will go to a special seminary for delayed vocations. Another person asked him why he was doing this and he replied, "Because I think it's what God wants me to do. I like the Navy but I feel I need to do something more meaningful. I can do a lot of good for a lot of people as a priest."

I wanted to explore the subject but thought I might do more harm than good. I wanted to point out the fact that sometimes a dedicated layperson can do far more good than a clergy person. But that's not the kind of thing he wanted to hear. But I'm not worried about you, dear reader, so here goes. First an allegory.

A farmer was converted at a revival meeting. His whole life took on a hyper tone. He knew a happiness he had not known before. One day while plowing he stopped to rest. Sitting against a tree, looking at the clouds, he saw them form two huge letters P and C. God was calling him, he was sure. What could the letters mean but *Preach Christ?* He sold his farm and went off to seminary where he proceeded to flunk every course. Very crestfallen he went to the dean. He explained his "call" and asked, "If God wanted me to be his minister, why isn't he helping me?" In his kindest voice the dean said, "Maybe you should re-think this. Maybe those letters meant "Plow corn."

Now let's look at a real case where a man did start out to be a minister but changed his mind. Keith Miller, in his classic *The Taste of New Wine,* tells of going to seminary, but being "called back out" to be a layperson. He would have been a great minister, but, he says, "Working in my vocation of management, mostly in the engineering and oil industries, I found many people coming to me for advice. They would say, 'I have a problem and there is something about you that makes me believe you could help.'"

He practices following Jesus. He doesn't preach about him, or seek ways to start conversations into which he can push his "message." Rather he is the block of salt to which persons in need come. If there they find Jesus, it's simply because that is where Jesus is.

In an unforseen way I round this to be true in my own life. I was ordained, a *man of the cloth.* I was *different.* People around me couldn't talk the same, play as good a game of golf, or be as comfortable with me when they discovered I was a minister. Reminds me of the time I went to State Conference and heard the announcement to the assembly from the chair: If you need to use the facilities they are one floor down. You'll find them plainly marked for men, women and clergy. We are sort of third sex I guess. When we do something good for humanity or act in some moral way, it is because we are supposed to be good. We're ministers. But when a layperson does the same things, it inspires other persons to emulate him or her and talk about those things. When I began teaching some twenty-two years ago, the change was startling. Students came to my office to talk in far greater numbers than did soldiers to the chapel when I was a chaplain or young people to my church office when I was a pastor. They knew I was of the clergy, but the fact that I was now a social scientist, brought them to me with questions they had held in for years.

We are all called, as Paul says in Ephesians *some to be pastors, some teachers, etc.* But if we feel the call to be a parish minister, we'd better take a lesson from the Reverend Will B. Dunn in the comic strip Kudzu. He had become discouraged by the ups and downs of parish administration. He thought of a clever way to shore up his courage. He started a rumor that he was thinking of suicide. He climbed to the top of the water tower and put one leg over. He saw a crowd gathering and said to himself, "This stunt to resurrect my ministry seems to be working." Then to his dismay he heard his congregation begin to call out from the ground way below, "Jump, jump, jump!"

The whole idea in following Christ is not to win a popularity contest; it's just to do the best we can with God's help. If we do this, to be or not to be a clergy person will make little difference.

I've Changed My Mind

What an odd expression, "I changed my mind!" When we say, "I changed the tire on the car," or "I changed my shirt," we mean we exchanged one thing for another. We can't exchange our mind—exchange it for what? Maybe what we mean is closer to "I changed channels on the TV." "I changed my mind," is an idiomatic expression—slightly different from idiotic expression. It is a peculiarity of the English language which gives foreigners fits when they are trying to understand us. What must a foreigner think when literally interpreting the phrase "her face fell?" Does she wait for the *thump* that must follow when the face hits the floor? Or when a foreign student reads "he cast his eyes out over the waters," does he wait for the inevitable *splash* that must follow?

Idiom means "peculiar to oneself or one's culture." Idioms are embedded too deeply in a language to allow change. I wouldn't want to change them anyway; they are a kind of colorful shorthand—mental pictures that speak a thousand words. Besides, they're too much fun. What would we do if we couldn't talk about women changing their minds? One woman laid that old saw to rest for all time. She was a suffragette speaking before the Kansas state legislators in 1920, seeking to gain the right to vote. A Senator remarked: "It would be a dangerous thing to do, give women the right to vote, seeing as how they change their minds so easily." She shot back: "I would like to ask the honorable senator if he ever tried to change a woman's mind once it has been made up?" That ended that!

People who easily change their minds are said to be open minded. The door is open and every new idea that comes along just walks in and makes itself at home. Sometimes they are so open minded that ideas just keep slipping off either end. Then there are those whose mental door is closed and a new idea hasn't been in for ages. They are said to be closed minded. Their slogan is "My mind is made up—don't confuse me with the facts. They have hardening of the categories.

You've seen them in your church; they believe fanatically in the Seven Last Words: WE NEVER DID IT THAT WAY BEFORE! I used to call such persons "Pillars of the Church." Pillars are used to hold up things and they hold up progress.

There have to be intelligent, normal, thoughtful people out there who can entertain data, evaluate them, compare them with their own mind set and either change their minds or cast aside the data. You know, people like me—and you. You see, I believe (my mind set) that God creates us with minds that are instruments to be used; instruments with which to build theories and to change theories; instruments with which to build societies and to change societies; instruments with which to build churches and to change churches; instruments with which to build lives and to change lives.

Using the minds God gave us in this fashion is scary to some people and when fear grips their minds they band together and defend their personal "orthodoxy" to the death. People who created the Flat Earth Society, for instance. It has over a thousand members to whom you cannot prove with any observations or logic that the earth is round. There are others who absolutely believe that the Holocaust never took place; they will tell you that it was a story fabricated by the Jews to serve their own purposes. And there are those who will never believe we landed a man on the moon. "It was all done with trick photography and television," they say. Well, don't try to wake them up. They'd never change their minds and would only resent you for disturbing them. They are "at ease in Zion." Leave 'em be.

As for me I like Paul's words in Philippians 2:5 *Have this mind in you which was in Christ Jesus.* I hope in some tiny measure that I have lived up to that. Jesus tried to change his countrymen's minds about healing people on the Sabbath, changing money in the temple and most of all about the Kingdom, which he said *Is already among you,* an idea about which the Pharisees would not change their minds. *Follow me* Jesus said, *all people will know that you are my disciples if you have love one for another.*

I don't think I'll change my mind about that.

Patience

In the comic strip Kudzu we see the preacher, Will B. Dunn kneeling in prayer. He is saying, "God, give me patience; and please, I need it now!"

Patience is a state of mind. It denotes the ability to calmly bear the "slings and arrows of outrageous fortune." When people display this capability they are often said to have "the patience of a saint." For some reason or other I get a negative feeling about this portrait of sainthood. It sort of reminds me of the familiar painting showing a farmer (with pitchfork in hand) and his wife, standing in front of their barn, waiting for the grain to ripen. Impatience is rather the order of the day for most people and I'm one of those people. Someone opined: He also serves who only stands and waits. I concede that this is true if he is standing in the on deck circle waiting to bat or is a stand-in hoping the star of the show will catch a cold, but waiting in general is not my ticket to sainthood. So I thought I'd write a homily to myself about patience and let you read it, too.

We wouldn't need patience if it weren't for frustration. Frustration is the negative feeling we get when our progress toward a goal is blocked. A slow driver in front of us when we're late for work, the ball game delayed on account of rain, the window in the bank is closed when we are next in line, etc. What we do about our frustrations influences our social portrait, our personality. We can either break rules and laws to get ahead faster, stepping on people along the way, or we can set goals and work toward them in a systematic way.

A parishioner went to her minister and said, "Pastor will you pray with me that I will have more patience?"

"Certainly," he said, "let's kneel." He began: "O Lord send some tribulations and hardships and difficulties to this thy child . . ."

She interrupted him with, "No, no, no! I have plenty of those. What I need is patience."

He said, "I'm only going along with St. Paul. He said to the Romans, 'Tribulation worketh patience and patience experience and experience hope.'" We can't any more learn how to handle frustration without experiencing it than we can learn to ride a bicycle by reading a book of instructions.

Frustration is a source of stress and stress can be debilitating to our physical system. Stomach problems, skin problems, heart problems, digestive problems, all can be caused by too much stress, and often the too much stress is due to our inability to cope with frustration. So what attitude do we take toward frustration that will put us on the road to a masters degree in coping? How do we become more like the diner who called the waiter. "Yes, sir. What do you wish?"

"Well," he said in a kindly manner, "I wished for breakfast quite a while ago and then more recently for lunch, but if dinner is ready I'll have it now." That's patience!

I heard another preacher say who arrived late for meeting, "I started to get in the car a while ago and saw that I had a flat tire. I felt frustration begin to rise, but I took the bull by the horns and opened the trunk of the car to get the spare and (you guessed it) the spare was flat. I began to perspire and felt my heart beat faster. Then it came to me—what would I advise my parishioners to do in a situation like this? So I knelt right there and asked God for help. I got a message. It seemed to be spoken aloud. 'What if you were on your way to the hospital with a dying child?' The light bulb went on. I called a taxi and here I am."

St Paul was right *Tribulation worketh patience and patience experience and experience hope.* That preacher is hoping such a thing never happens again. The next time you or I are faced with a tribulation let us pray **not** "Why have you got it in for me, God?" Rather let us pray, "What have you got in this for me, God?" And maybe add, "And send a few more tribulations to the Reverend Will B. Dunn. Amen."

O Death, Where Is Thy Sting?

In a Russell Myers' comic strip *Broom Hilda*, Irwin, the porcupine, is at the mailbox, reading a letter that just arrived. He says to Witch Hilda, riding by on her broom, "My Uncle Whootley died last week."

"That's too bad, Irwin," said Hilda, "was it a surprise?"

"I suppose so," said Irwin, "it never happened to him before."

Northern Essex Community college did not have a course on death and dying—it never happened to them before. Because of some experiences in my life I wanted to know more about the subject that is kept under wraps. And I thought if I wanted to, maybe there would be others who would like to join me, so I started the course called Death and Dying. It was oversubscribed from the start. Though people don't want to discuss the subject over coffee and around the water cooler, they want to legitimately delve into its mysteries.

Immediately people began asking me, "Why in the world do you want to teach a course like that?" I could only say, "Because I want to learn more about it myself."

Many people don't want to learn anything more about the subject than they know already. My grandmother had a simple but adequate knowledge of the subject: *if you live a bad life you go to hell; if you lead a good life you go to heaven.* As the little girl put it, "I think heaven will be the happiest part of my dead life." Very simple!

But after many years as a pastor and chaplain in the army, I had a need for a more satisfactory understanding of death. I had the haunting thought that maybe—just maybe—death didn't have to be as much of a surprise as it was to Irwin's uncle. What follows is a part of the prologue to a book I wrote during the teaching of that course. The title of the book is *Death and Life.*

The door, closed, "Let me have your hat and coat, Pastor."

It was my first parish. I sat down to discuss the funeral service for Patty, their eight-year-old daughter. I can't remember what I said, but I remember how I felt—anxious. My whole body was tight. My mind was racing to find the right word to say and to hold back the slip of the tongue that might cause pain. When I left I felt I had failed, though later they told me I had helped. I thought: *The teachers at the seminary hadn't taught me single thing about this!* And they hadn't.

Two years later. The tockety-tockety-whoosh of the copter blades—the hurried footsteps and labored breathing of the medics as they transferred the wounded from the "coffins" (as they called the coverings for the stretchers on the side of the copters) to the A & D tent. We were in the MASH unit in Whachon, Korea. Copter after copter came and the stretchers were laid in neat rows as the doctors and nurses quietly and efficiently assessed the nature of the wounds, gave medications, and attached disposition tags (designating to which of the surgical teams each soldier would go). Then came my turn. 0h how I wished I could be as effective as the medical staff. I held a hand, talked if they were conscious, prayed if they desired it, but thought again: *I was never prepared for anything like this.* And I wasn't.

Several years later. Now the pastor of a church south of Boston. The young people of the church were at an outing. A sixteen-year-old boy, good swimmer, drowned when he tried to swim out to an island. I had to inform the parents. I went to the house. They were not home. I sat in my car waiting agonizing moments; I was rehearsing. I was thinking what to say, how I would say it, and how I would start, how I would leave, how I would stand or sit, none of which seemed adequate. Again I don't know what I said exactly, or what occurred. I know I had to be alone awhile afterwards, devastated by the death of this beautiful young person and by my feeling of helplessness. No one prepared me for this.

I became convinced that of all the critical times in a person's life, the time of one's own death or the death of a loved one is the most profound, the most anguishing, and yet the most meaning-full time. This was where education should start. I needed to learn about my own mortality (Latin for deathness), and my own finiteness (Latin for destined to end, limited). I learned some of this during the years I was earning my P H. D. degree in counseling and psychotherapy, but I think learned the most from parishioners and friends who were dying and from their bereaved families. I did not learn any magic words to say to the dying and bereaved. There aren't any.

I did learn that dying is a physiological, intellectual, emotional, and social process; that it is closely connected to the experience of separation and loss, any separation or loss; that it involves the process of relinquishing in order to truly possess; that it is inextricably intertwined with life and love.

I learned that the process of dying begins when we lose the "safety" and "comfort" of the womb, continues with our loss of childhood, toys, pets, schools, parents, homes, and so on till we at last relinquish our work, our relationships, and ultimately our body.

I learned, too, that we never gain something without relinquishing something; never come to a beginning without an ending (that's why graduation is called commencement); never truly love until we first discard possessiveness. All of nature's living systems are really living-dying systems. A seed must die to produce a flower; a flower must die to produce a seed; something must die for us to be fed and nourished and kept alive; we must die to make room for our replacements, The words "life" and "death" have no fundamental meaning apart from each other.

The truly living person is the one who understands and accepts his dying. The truly dead person is the one who refuses to accept, who suppresses and denies his dying. The living person is freed from the fear and denial of death. There is an aliveness, a growing, an enthusiasm (Latin for *entheos*: God within). The dead person is vegetating, stagnant, unenthusiastic, is in short, "in a rut." It has been humorously put that a rut is only a grave with both ends knocked out.

I hope all this learning will stand me in good stead until the day that Irwin, the porcupine, will say of me, "It never happened to him before."

Singing at Midnight

A recent book *Positive Illusions*, by Shelley E. Taylor, supports a view I have held for many years. She says *we are in charge of our feelings*. Such a statement is enough to make many readers close the book. It seems more often like *our feelings are in charge of us*. A loved one dies, we lose our job, depression grips our spirits. Is Shelley Taylor really saying that even in such times *you are in charge of your feelings*? Let's give her a little wiggle room. She is saying that we are not prisoners of our feelings. We can still choose to ***do*** something though it be a struggle. The Children of Israel had been taken captive to Babylon—as slaves—and there asked to entertain the Babylonians with some of their beautiful songs. *How can we sing the Lord's song in a strange land*, they said and hung their harps in the willow trees. But they could do one thing. They could remember Jerusalem, and so they did. The popular song had it right, I think: "The memories of love will see me through."

Sometimes, Like Garfield, we wake up and say, "Mondays have it in for me." We are not quite sure why we feel down but we think we "should of stood in bed." But Are we puppets? Must we be dominated by external events or be captive to our juices? Do we have any part at all to play in just how blue or sad we feel? Shelley Taylor says yes and she offers all kinds of proof. I have told my classes to force a smile when they are down in the dumps. "Whistle while you work," as it were. Mental and physical well-being can be measurably enhanced by seemingly unrealistic but positive kinds of behavior.

I think of Paul and Silas sitting in the Philippian Jail at midnight, feet in irons and backs bleeding and smarting from the whipping they had endured because they preached Christ on the street corner. If anyone had a right to be discouraged and blue, they had. I can imagine Silas feeling his sore back and then examining his hand. "Look, Paul," he says, "blood." Paul reaches around and feels his back, looks at the blood on his hand and says, "Yeah, me too. Let's sing." And the Bible tells us that "they sang hymns at midnight." As they sang the walls of the prison came tumbling down. It is never easy when we feel shackled and the lights of our life go out and we sit in the dark. But just start humming: "Amazing Grace, how sweet the sound," or "Precious

Lord, Hold My Hand" and see if the space around you does not get brighter—see if your limbs feel less shackled.

I've always loved the gospel spirituals arising from the slave days. They affirm this truth. Many slaves would certainly have perished had they not sung in spite of the pain, the darkness and the shackles. I heard a widow say soon after the death of her loved one, "When somebody asks me how I feel, I'm going to tell a fib. I'm going to force a smile and say, 'I feel fine,' even though I don't, and I'm going to keep saying it until I feel better again."

This does not mean we should not share our pain with those who are good friends and really want to listen. It means that our physical and mental systems respond positively to optimistic outlooks, even when we feel least like being positive. As God tells us through Isaiah, "A bruised reed he will not break."

And the Christian, especially, has a power greater than the power of drugs or psychotherapy, The Master says *Come unto me, all you who are hurting and I will give you rest.* I think that is what my grandmother knew. She had many troubles of which I, as a little boy, was unaware. I can still hear her singing "I must tell Jesus all of my trials, I cannot bear these burdens alone; In my distress he kindly will help me, He always loves and cares for his own." I could not see the blackness of her midnight or the blood on her back or the prison walls around her, but looking back now I'm pretty sure that when she sang, the prison walls came tumbling down.

I Think that I Shall Never See . . .

One of my favorite comic strips is "For Better or Worse." On one occasion the family was putting up the Christmas tree and little Elizabeth asked with excited anticipation, "Can I help put on the desecrations?" We laugh and say, "Ridiculous but funny." But is it so ridiculous? Read the following and then reassess your judgments.

Some missionaries to a treeless, desert land had a bright idea about celebrating Christmas with the natives who knew nothing of our traditions; they had a live fir tree air-shipped from the United States along with some bulbs and tinsel. At night, while all the natives were asleep, they decorated the tree with tinsel, red and green balls, silver icicles, etc. They got up early and sat watching expectantly as the natives trooped in one by one ready for work and classes. They all stood speechless, staring at this strange thing they knew nothing about. The missionaries had them sit by the tree as they described to the wide-eyed group the celebrations that were going on back home at this very hour. It seemed like the natives were quite impressed. Late that night one of the missionaries saw a light in the chapel and went to put it out. He was more surprised by what he saw than any of the natives had been that morning. They had stripped the tree of every single ornament and were sitting around it in wide-eyed wonder. They had got rid of the "desecrations," as Elizabeth called them in the comic strip. They had never seen a tree and the tree was more beautiful to them than the decorations.

This "desecration" doesn't bother me—in fact I like it—but there is another one that does bother; it is the humongous pile of presents under the tree. A gift is nice. It is exciting, it means a lot to the receiver and the one who gave it, the one who thought about it and spend time looking for just the right thing. Gifts—receiving and getting—beget a warm, friendly, joyous atmosphere that is such a wonderful part of Christmas. So how could gifts be a desecration? I guess it's the profusion of them; they speak of opulence, and opulence always seems to be so out of place at the celebration of Jesus' birth—especially in a world where hundreds of children will die Christmas night for want of enough bread to eat.

Our family decided to do something about it this year. We followed the example of some other families we knew and drew names. We agreed to give one gift to the person whose name we drew. The department stores and malls will think we are being un-American, but if we take some of the money we don't spend for presents and send it to CARE, Oxfam America, AmeriCares or another favorite charity, I think we will feel a larger sense of wonder and awe and a smaller sense of "desecration" this Christmas.

Another desecration happens in our churches. I dare say that very few who read these words will have given it much thought, or even that much could be done about it if they had, at least not in a short period of. time. I'll illustrate it with a true story and leave you to contemplate its meaning. William Stidger, a teacher of mine in seminary, author, newspaper columnist, preacher, had some feelings about the desecration of Christmas and decided to teach a lesson about it. He let his beard grow several days, got some worn jeans, a ragged overcoat and crumpled hat and started out to worship at a midnight Christmas Eve service in a Boston church. He approached and asked if there was a Christmas eve service there. As he expected he was told of a mission church where he would probably feel more at home. The same experience was repeated at several other churches.

The next day he was scheduled to speak at the Christmas Morning Service at the Goodwill Industries Chapel. He entered the church and sat in a back pew, unrecognized. The leaders of the service got more and more nervous as the time to start came and went. Stidger sat for several minutes till he knew his entrance would get the most attention. Then this tramp-like man came down the aisle, strode to the pulpit, and told his experience of the night before trying to celebrate the Christ Child's birth in several Christian churches, but there was no room at the inn.

Thank you, Elizabeth, for making me think about this. May your Christmas tree be beautifully desecrated and your family mightily "blessicated" this year.

"Music Hath Charms"

One young man said to his family, "I'm going away to study music." The unanimous reply was, "Good! How far away?" That didn't happen to me exactly—only because I couldn't *afford* to go away. As I look back I'm surprised my family didn't take up a collection to help me go away, like the instructor said to his less-than-brilliant singing student, "Sing by the open window and I'll help you out." You can see that my own appreciation for my singing talent varied somewhat from that of my family.

From an early age I wanted to study music; I used to listen to the popular singing evangelists that sang in our church and at camp meetings and I wanted to be one of them in the worst way (which is the way it turned out to be). I took singing lessons when I got into my teens. I saved some money from my job in a cafeteria and found a teacher by looking in the Yellow Pages. She tried to help me with my goal, I'm sure, but she never actually encouraged me much. She should have told me, "Go home and be good to your mother," but I guess she needed the money. The nearest thing to encouragement was when she told me I should raise my vocal range and become a tenor. I tried! I picked away at the old piano in our basement at 1717 B Street in Washington, DC . . . "La-bay-dah-may-nee-po-tu" in C then "la-bay-dah-may-nee-po-tu" in C-sharp, then "la-bay-da-may-nee-po-too" in D and up and up till I was screeching. My poor mother! I gave up on the tenor bit and all other singing bits and settled for singing for the rest of my life in the "also" range. But I learned a lot along the way. I learned that under my rib cage was a muscle called the diaphragm and that it was supposed to help me "project;" that I was to consider the tones as a column of air being forced up and bouncing off the roof of my mouth; that I should listen for vibrations in my chest; and that I should be the best me I could be and stop trying to be someone else. Ill have to say this for my family, though: they didn't try to discourage me. But then they didn't *encourage* me either.

Music is a universal language. Every culture expresses itself in rhythm and words. Rhythm and words—right hemisphere and left hemisphere of the brain. Language in the left cerebral cortex; timing, tunes and rhythm in the right. When people have a stroke that affects the left hemisphere of the brain, they lose words—language. It is agonizing for them when they try to speak and embarrassing for a friend who tries to understand them. They can't find the words. But somehow, it you play them a tune they can remember the words—their eyes light up—miracle! Perhaps that is why we are often lifted to such heights when singing or listening to a great hymn: both sides of the brain are united—a gulf is bridged that raises us above the everyday struggle to interpret our world. A story apropos to this comes out of World War I.

A company of soldiers was securing a village following the retreat of the German army. They were told to proceed with utmost caution, not to enter buildings alone and above all not to fraternize with the citizens of the town. One lieutenant, passing a church, could not resist entering and looking around. He saw an organ and something stirred in him. He had been the organist for his Methodist church back home before the war began. He thought it wouldn't hurt to just sit down and play a bit before going on. He started playing *Ein' Feste Burg*, "A Mighty Fortress is Our God." Softly he played at first then louder and louder as he got carried away. Suddenly he heard voices. He heard the words being sung. He looked around and saw twenty-five or thirty German people who had wandered in, one by one, to the attraction of the music. They were young, old, male, female, well-dressed, poor. He stood up, embarrassed, not knowing just what to do in the situation. Then an old man solved the dilemma. He walked forward with open arms saying, "Mein bruder, mein bruder," and they embraced. Yes *Music hath charms to soothe the savage breast; To soften rocks, or bend a knotted oak."*

I can think of some people in my church who need bending. Maybe there's a lesson here.

Christmas Eve in Kumhwa

There were only the stars to give light. We could not use headlights or flashlights. Even a candle could be seen forty miles away on a clear night like this. My driver and I were on our way to an artillery position near Khumwa in Korea. I was the chaplain and was bringing the men in that outfit a Christmas Eve service. I was leaning out the right side of the Jeep watching the road while my driver was leaning out the left. The roads were narrow, full of ruts and ran close to an occasional ditch or ravine which we held our breath trying to avoid. The dim light of the odometer told us we were near the outpost and we were certain about it when we heard the click of a rifle bolt and a "Halt!" from the sentry (whom we had not seen). After satisfying himself that we were OK, he helped us find our way to the motor pool and then to the tent in which the service was to be held. We entered through the light trap and emerged into warmth and light and some Christmas music coming out of a tape machine. I looked about in amazement as I took off my parka, helmet, earmuffs, double mittens and scarf. What those lonely boys had done to make that old tent in the middle of nowhere look something like Christmas brought tears to my eyes. There were candles and there was a scrubby shrub decorated with paper decorations they had made.

My driver set up the little altar and we distributed the small, red, army hymnals. No service I was ever in was richer in meaning than that one. No carols were ever sung with more feeling. After the homily, the prayers and the singing we all shared our thoughts about what was going on back home, who was at who's house, what their relatives would be eating and who would be opening gifts.

For some reason, after that service, I decided not to return to base camp just yet. I walked carefully through the dark to the FDC (fire direction center), wondering whether any military action was taking place on this, the night of our Savior's birth. In the FDC there were large flat tables with maps on them. Men were using triangulation devices to locate the position of the FO (forward observer), the artillery pieces and the approximate position of the "enemy." The radio was alive with the usual information from the FOs. Then began one of the strangest Christmas stories you can imagine. An FO, looking through an infrared scope, reported several enemy soldiers coming down from the hills across the valley. They seemed to be carrying a package. They set the package down and went back.

The men at the tables figured the approximate position of the activity. Presently the same observation was made. Two more soldiers came into the valley with a package. "Shall we send in some rounds?" asked the FO. The commanding officer said, "No, let's wait." This went on till there were a dozen large boxes in the middle of the valley. Then from the hills on the other side of the valley came the strains of "Silent Night, Holy Night." Other carols were played by the enemy soldiers for about an hour. Nothing else occurred that night. The next day the packages were recovered, opened and were found to contain real gifts. They were plain and inexpensive, but obviously meant as gifts. There was much discussion as to the meaning of what went on. Most thought it was psychological warfare, making our soldiers so homesick that they would desert. I'll never know but I still wonder. After all this was one of the few nights when there were no soldiers either killed or missing in action. Two thousand years before, the Prince of Peace was born into a world where there was darkness and war and strife. There was singing and lights and gifts on that night, too, and as far as I know, no soldiers were killed on that night either.

The Bridge That Carries You Across

I was in a taxi in New York City. The cabby was whistling. I said, "How can you be so happy in such a stressful job?"

He replied: "I wasn't always happy. Was a time I wanted to quit so bad I got ulcers. I felt like this was a flunky job. I wanted to have a job like the people have who ride in my cab. I wanted to be able to dress like they do. I wanted to whistle and have a cab stop for me and carry me across town. Then one day when I was grousing to my mother she said, 'Son, never cuss the bridge that carries you across.' I got to thinkin'. I was married; we had two kids; we was eatin' and had a roof, and I began to feel better. Now I have two kids through college. My mother was right."

I knew I had my sermon for the next Sunday. That was forty years ago. I hope that sermon helped some person to reassess the things in his or her life that are getting them through, things they sometimes gripe about and pray to God for relief about. It has stuck with me all these years, and when I find myself wishing I was getting ahead faster I say to myself, *Never cuss the bridge that carries you across.*

That's short and sweet and doesn't need a lot of supportive rhetoric. Reminds me of the little boy who asked, "Mom, where did I come from?" The mother gulped, her palms started to sweat and her heart sped up a bit. She thought, "I knew it would come some day and I guess this is it!" She sat down with him on the couch and began a long lecture on the birds and the bees. After about ten minutes he interrupted her with: "I know all that stuff, Mom, but Jimmy comes from Philadelphia and I want to know where I come from." So you can stop reading here and forget the rest of the stuff if you like. But being a preacher I have to throw in some illustrations. If you are one who can't leave anything half read, stick with me for a few more paragraphs.

Never cuss your bridge? How about "*Most of the time* don't cuss the bridge?" I think of the Bridge of Sighs in Venice. The span across which inmates were led from the prison to the Ducal Palace where they were to stand trial. Or how about *The Bridge of San Luis Rey*, the most famous bridge in Peru? In 1714 the bridge collapsed hurling five people to their deaths in the gorge below. But those are real, physical bridges. The bridge the cabby's mother was thinking about was a metaphor for life. It was said in another way by the old man in Vermont when a visitor asked him: "What's it like to be so old?" The old native said, "Way-ul, considerin' the alternative . . . ." I guess it's as simple as that—and as profound.

So as RMN used to say while shaking his jowls, "Let me say this about that." The bridge we are speaking of is hope. The Samaritans often ask a caller, "Why have you not committed suicide already?" Sounds cruel and risky, doesn't it? But think what it does. The person reaches down inside himself and finds a reason—child, grandchild, something unfinished, whatever. And however small that something is, it can be a basis for hope. On such small beginnings one can construct a bridge leading back to life and meaning. Paul wrote about faith, hope and love and proclaimed that the greatest of the three was love. Maybe he was wrong. Maybe the greatest of these is hope—the bridge between the other two.

Maybe the bridge that really carries us across is hope.

The Salt of the Earth

When I was a kid on the farm, I never thought much about salt. In fact, the only time I can remember thinking about it at all was when I went with Grandpa Parsons to replace a block of salt in the pasture. I think I asked him what it was and he told me how cows had to have it or they would die. Somehow I didn't equate the needs of cows and my needs. I knew I liked it, and I knew it made a piece of raw potato taste real good, but I didn't know I'd die if deprived of it.

But lately I have learned that we all contain three to four salt cellars of this magic substance in our bodies, and we must constantly be replacing it, for we keep losing it in small amounts through sweat, tears, saliva, and larger amounts in that other liquid.

I know that table salt is a combination of sodium and chlorine called sodium chloride. But if I knew, I had forgotten that sodium is an unstable metal that can burst into flame unpredictably and burn anyone handling it, and that chlorine is a deadly poisonous gas which could kill us if inhaled, yet combined they become table salt, a sustainer of life. *Oh, Lord, our Lord, how magnificent is thy name in all the earth!*

When Jesus said to his disciples, *you are the salt of the earth; but if salt has lost its taste, how shall its saltiness be restored? It is no longer good for anything except to be thrown out and trodden under foot,* he gave preachers wide latitude to interpret the meaning of his words

Perhaps he meant "You are valuable." Salt was a costly necessity. It was the medium of exchange for thousands of years. The roman soldiers were given a paycheck called a salarium, which meant simply "salt money," money with which to buy salt. It is from this that our word salary comes.

Or maybe he meant "You are the true flavor of life," for above all other qualities, salt is desired for its enhancement of flavor. Wouldn't it be great if people wanted Christians around because their joy, their zest for life, and their moral behavior lent a happy prospect to any group? Unfortunately history has sometimes pictured "Christians" as dour and glum. In the days of the Pilgrims it was considered a sin to laugh on Sunday. Even preachers have a hand in this. On July 8, 1871 the powerful evangelist, Jonathan Edwards, preached a sermon that made a whole generation shake in their boots. It was called, "Sinners In the Hands of an Angry God," and pictured the unsaved as hanging by a slender thread over the everlasting fires of hell. Oliver Wendell Holmes once said, "I gave thought to becoming a minister, but the ones I knew looked and acted so much like undertakers, I thought again." And Robert Louis Stevenson entered in his diary: "I attended church today, and to my surprise, I'm not depressed."

We need to bring back the radiance, the sparkle and joy that make real Christians the salt of the earth.

Salt once brought a "preservative" influence into my life. I was about nine years old, had just moved to a new school and of course, as newcomer, was the butt of harassment and teasing. It hurt a lot. Then Mom got a letter from John Windemiller, a sailor she had known in younger days. Now that she was a widow he was courting her. He said something about salt and a salt cellar which I misunderstood and thought he ate whole cellars of salt and promptly told my schoolmates. It helped a little. John Windemiller became my Dad. I adopted his name when I became of age. It was terrible to lose my genetic father, but what a break to get one like Jack White the Fighting Sailor, as he was called. He taught me to row a boat, tie knots and fish. He was a little mean sometimes, making me do dishes and sweep the floor, etc. But when the need was greatest, he was there. He once sent me to pick up a gear bag after a boxing match. The Janitor threw me out. My father went up to the man, grabbed him by his shirt front, put him up against the wall and said, "When I send my son for something, you give it to him!"

He might have been an old salt, but to me, and I think to Jesus, too, he was the salt of the earth.

Holy Juice

A mother in Greensboro, NC—also a pastor—was fixing a lunch for her little daughter and some friends. She gave them potato chips and Juicy-Juice. The juice apparently reminded the daughter of communion for she started to recite the words she had heard her mother say so often. Her mother was amazed at how much her daughter had absorbed. She came to the closing prayer of the service. Everything had gone amazingly accurate, till she ended with the words, "In the name of the Father, the Son and the holy juice."

Holy juice. Did you ever wonder how grape juice got to be "holy?" Would you like to hear it? You're going to anyway.

Doctor Thomas Welch was the Communion Steward for the congregation of the First Methodist Church of Vineland, New Jersey, in 1869. During that summer, to his great dismay, the communion wine used by the church became a bit too fermented and set some of the communicants on a binge. Determined to do something about this, he and his family spent the following September picking and pressing about forty pounds of grapes. In an attempt to repress the natural fermentation properties in the fruit, he heated the juice, pasteurizing it before sealing it in bottles. For the next few weeks he listened anxiously for the sounds of exploding bottles, but nothing happened. When Welch opened the containers, he found nothing but sweet, unfermented grape juice. Dubbed "unfermented wine," this beverage was an instant hit. After introducing it to his own church, Dr. Welch began selling it to various other congregations and denominations. By 1890 "Dr. Welch's Grape Juice" had become a staple on communion tables, where for many congregations it remains so today.

The communion beverage is holy only as the partaker of it senses it in his or her heart. Here is how one person achieved this inner sense of "holy" juice.

Walter Wangerin, Jr., son of a clergyman, wrote an insightful book about the concepts of childhood *Little Lamb, Who Made Thee?* In it he tells of his relentless examination of every nook and cranny of his father's church, trying to find where Jesus hid. One Sunday he sat beside his mother in church. It was communion Sunday. His mother went to the front to receive the elements. Walter did not know what she was doing. When she came back he kept whispering questions. "What did you do?" "Why did you go?" "What was that you ate?" She tried to tell him to keep him quiet and finally settled on, "That was Jesus. I ate Jesus." "So that's where he hides," thought little Walter. What better place? His mother was the holiest thing he knew. Where else would Jesus hide? With that he snuggled up close to her, as near to Jesus as he could get.

Everyone has feelings about communion, based on their experiences growing up. I can imagine Walter Wangerin will have a sense a wonderment about it few others have. Another little boy I encountered was quite dumb struck by the concept of taking the body and blood of Jesus into his body. He was taking first communion instructions from the Catholic chaplain in a military chapel at Fort Bragg, NC. I was waiting for the chaplain to be finished so we could play golf. There was a protestant boy, friend of the one taking lessons, also waiting. When the class was over the little students marched out. The Protestant boy said to his friend, "What did you learn?" and the Catholic boy answered, "You wouldn't believe it!" Not a bad interpretation of the whole concept of communion. For most of my life I have served holy juice to the churches I have served, but while in the army as a chaplain the protocol was communion wine. In 1951 in Korea the Catholic chaplain and I would travel to the outposts of the 102nd Artillery Group taking communion to the troops. Chaplain Chehayle would ride in the front beside the driver because he was a major and I was only a captain—rank has its privileges—and believe me it was a privilege as any one would know who had ridden over potholed roads in the back of a Jeep. Ouch!

When we arrived, Father Chehayle would get out the communion chest, take out the cloths and brass symbols and turn the hood of the Jeep into a Catholic altar. The Catholic troops would leave the guns, gather around the Jeep—pardon me, the altar—receive communion, listen to a short homily, then return to the guns. Then I took some different brass accouterments, turning the vehicle into a Protestant Jeep, and proceeded to conduct a communion service. One thing was different about my service. We sang hymns. The army provided a hymnal chest to every protestant chaplain. The wee, red hymnals held only about one hundred hymns, the most familiar, but I think that singing the old hymns after communion added some meaning to the "holy" of the holy juice.

Some of the Catholic boys would come over and join in the singing. I don't know what Father Chehayle thought of it. I never discussed that with him.

Rotated to Japan in 1952, I was stationed at camp McNair for six weeks. Camp McNair was 8,000 feet up on the side of Mt. Fujiama, a 12,000 foot volcanic mountain. From the hood of a Jeep in Korea I was now switched to a Quonset hut. At least there were chairs, an altar and a lectern. There was even a small pump organ that made it easier to sing hymns—if we could find a soldier who could play it.

Now I sat in my small office in the Quonset hut and waited for the Catholic Chaplain to finish Mass before the Protestant men had their service. I practically learned the Mass by heart—I heard it so many times. One thing I found amusing: The last thing the Catholic chaplain said in his service was, "The Mass is ended." The soldiers, reading from the missal, or reciting by heart, would say, "Praise be to God." I think Protestants could take a cue here. When the preacher finishes his sermon and says, "Amen," the congregation should say, "Praise be to God."

And so as I serve communion now, the table, whatever kind it might be, stretches around the world and somehow mysteriously becomes one with the table around which Jesus and the disciples sat. It is an invisible connection between Jesus and the vast numbers of his disciples. You will have your mental picture of the hands that have been with yours around communion tables of the past as they lift up and drink the holy juice.

God the Magician

When I was a boy I thought magic was the greatest thing in the world. I am still fascinated by it. I wouldn't make a good magician, though, because I can't help explaining how A trick works. Reminds me of the parrot that belonged to a magician who's job was entertaining the passengers of a cruise line. The parrot sat on the magician's shoulder during his act. He was very observant and would sometimes ruin the act by saying, "The rabbit is under his coat," or "The card is up his sleeve." One day while doing his act the ship sank. All took to a life-raft. For days they drifted, the parrot looking intently at the magician all the while. Finally the parrot said, "Okay, I give up. What did you do with the ship?"

Miracles and magic have a lot in common. They both seem to suspend the laws of nature. Yet in our hearts we know that both can be explained. I sometimes use little magic tricks during the children's talk in church. I put a handkerchief over my outstretched palm and put a toothpick in the middle. Then I fold the sides of the handkerchief over the toothpick and tell one child to break it. They feel the break and hear it snap. I ask one of them to blow on it. Then I unfold the handkerchief and lo and behold the toothpick is still whole and unbroken. What a look on their faces! I wish I could get such a response from a sermon. But then I tell them about the toothpick hidden in the hem of the handkerchief and that was the one they broke. (See, I told you I couldn't help explaining my tricks!)

Then I talk with them about miracles. "No one, not even a doctor, knows how a cut on our finger knits back together. God knows, and some day when we are a lot smarter, he'll explain it. No one knows what makes a seed sprout up to become a tomato or a rose, not even the farmer. But God knows and someday he will tell us."

A letter from one little girl in Marshall & Hample's book *More Children's Letters to God*" said "Dear God, When it didn't rain I was sure my violets would not come up. But then they came up anyway. What you did was pretty good. Love, Betty." When I look out the window and contemplate the mighty ocean that's been there for some billions of years, and watch a sea gull bobbing on the waves, certain that the ocean was put there just for him (while all the time I know it was put there for me). And I drink in the colors of God's artistry among the trees on the fall hillside. It's all magic! It's all miracles!

"Dear God, what you did was pretty good."

Love,
Duane.

Knowing Where the Rocks Are

Three clergymen were fishing together. They got to discussing their beliefs about the miracles of Jesus. Two were agreed that the miracle stories had been added later—that Jesus was just a great teacher and perfect man. This made the third preacher hot under the collar. "I'm not hanging around with two so-called Christians who are nothing but infidels," and with that he got out of the boat and walked ashore.

"Look at that!" said one of the two in the boat, "no wonder he believes in the miracles of Jesus. He can do 'em himself. He just walked on water!"

"Naw," said the other, that was no miracle. "He just knows where the rocks are."

Like many things in life, rocks can be positive or negative, healthful or hurtful. The same rocks that got the clergyman to shore might rip a hole in the underside of the fishermen's boat.

First let's examine a couple of good rocks.

Consider David's plea to the Lord in his time of stress *Hear my cry, O God; listen to my prayer . . . I call, for my heart grows faint; lead me to the rock that is higher than I.* [Psalm 61:1-2]

Like the little girl who asked her father if she could ride on his shoulders. "Tired of walking?" he asked. "No, I just like to be high enough above things to see them."

She needed perspective and that's what David needed. Feeling low and weak and insignificant, he needed to get high enough above things to see them.

He needed to climb on the shoulders of God, look around and get his bearings again

Note in the psalm that David was praying. What are you and I doing when we pray but asking to be led to the rock that is higher than we—to be carried on the shoulders of God? Later on, this same rock which comforted David, pushed up through the oceans of history and became the Rock of Ages. Upon this rock millions have found a sure foundation for their lives.

Around 1813 one young man, Edward Mote, found this Rock of Ages at a revival in London and later wrote the hymn that has "rocked" many a hymn sing,

My hope is built on nothing less
Than Jesus' blood and righteousness;
I dare not trust the sweetest frame,
But wholly lean on Jesus' name.
On Christ the solid rock I stand;
All other ground is sinking sand.

Mote became the pastor of the Strict Baptist Church of Sussex and remained till he was seventy-six. He was so influential there that at one point the congregation wanted to deed the church property to him. "No," he said, "just give me the pulpit and when I can no longer preach Christ from it, turn me out of that!"

I'm sure Pastor Mote preached about the other kind of rocks, too, the dangerous rocks of life, He must have preached many times about the Tempter's snares that would pull us off the Rock of Ages, snares like idiolatry, dishonesty, adultery, covetousness, etc. Any one of these could tear a hole in our ship of life. The Christian life is a struggle to avoid these perilous rocks and the Bible goes to great lengths to identify them—the Ten Commandments, for instance—and when we know where they are, to stay as far from them as possible.

Even preachers need to stay closer to the Rock of Ages than the rocks of temptation. One minister was preaching on the Ten Commandments. When he came to number seven he paused and said to himself, "Now I know where I left my bicycle."

There's another temptation not in the Commandments. It's the lure of the comfort and security we find on the shoulders of God. We are tempted to become religious hermits in order to avoid sin. But I believe we, if we are to earn our place on the Rock, must become a piece of the Rock, to give comfort and direction to others who are hurting and hopeless. Even as parents we do this.

There was a little girl coming home from school and being harassed by some mischievous boys who taunted her, pulled off her hat and tried to snatch her lunch pail. In tears she said as she ran, "I'll tell my mommy, I'll tell my mommy!" Then as she neared her house she looked up and there on the steps stood her mother. She stopped, turned and, flailing her lunch pail, she ran at the boys crying, "No I won't; here I come! No I won't; here I come!" And the boys ran.

We can be that too, not only to our children, but others who know us—a piece of the rock. When they see us or remember us, they can face life and say, "No I won't! Here I come!" We can do it because "we've been there, done that." We can give them a leg up to sit with us on the shoulders of God.

Dear God, I Quote

I was standing at parade rest in the central park of Fall River, Massachusetts, along with several hundred soldiers of the 102nd Artillery Group. I was their chaplain. The Memorial Day festivities began with an invocation read by one of the city's clergymen. His prayer was eloquent and I was following his words and praying with him in my heart when suddenly my attention was riveted to a phrase ". . . and let us proceed with the same faith and trust of Abraham of old who [and I quote] *went out not knowing where he was to go!*" I heard no more. My mind was taken up with the implications of quoting the scriptures to God, their author.

The clergyman was trying to do two things at the same time; he was trying to reach the heart of God in prayer and he was also trying to reach the hearts of the people with his eloquence. This is the awesome task that anyone takes on when praying to God in the name of, and in the presence of God's people.

I was once made acutely aware of this dilemma while visiting one of my parishioners at the hospital. She had a visitor so I said, "I'll drop in later," but the patient said, "Oh, no! Stay! I was just telling Mabel what wonderful bedside prayers you make. Show her, will you?" I can tell you, that was one difficult prayer to make!

The Fall River clergyman was doing what my parishioner was demanding of me, *showing us* he could make beautiful prayers. After that prayer in the park I began to take more notice of the public prayers I heard. Following are some of the types of prayers I heard.

The shopping list prayer starts with sick and needy in the parish, the needs of the church and its many programs and services, proceeds to the needs of the town, the state, the nation and the world. It was difficult to keep my mind on the praying. I don't know who stopped listening first, me or God.

The *scolding prayer* goes "O God, thou knowest there are those here who should be teachers in the Sunday School and there are those who should be reading their Bibles more, etc."

The *spigot prayer* is not organized, is not scolding anyone; it's simply talking at God. The spigot is turned on with "Dear God," and continues for what seems like a suitable time, then it is turned off with, "Amen." Shakespeare described it well when he wrote, "If my wind were but long enough to say my prayers, I would repent."

I'm told there is an *announcement prayer*, though I never heard one. I guess it would be like the benediction an old Quaker was heard giving: "God, thou knowest there is plenty of food for those who wish to stay after the service, and also plenty of hay for their horses. Amen."

I became convinced that public prayer needed a new dynamic, an infusion of reality. By coincidence (defined as a small miracle in which God chooses to remain anonymous) Polly and I attended a week-long session of Camps Farthest Out. Frank Lauback was the camp leader. What a privilege to spend a week in the company of that great man. I learned much about relaxation, meditative prayers, bodily movement prayers and especially visual prayers. We would envision ourselves walking in the fields with Jesus as he was teaching, or tossing our prayers for peace toward Russia, or hanging on a clothesline, getting limper and limper as one after another the clothespins of life let go till we were flying in the breeze, God's breeze.

The first thing I did when we got back was to start a prayer group in which we could experiment with differing dynamics of prayer. Shortly thereafter I was in my study when a couple came in. Three days earlier their baby girl was born in the South Weymouth Hospital. The baby couldn't eat. The best doctors were consulted. The child was dying. They said, "Maybe God can do something. That's why we came to you. Can you help us?" I said, "Can you let her go? Can you really put her completely in God's hands?" They said they could. I said, "Keep praying and especially tomorrow night when the prayer group meets at seven o'clock." I had an idea.

The next evening I told the group about the problem. I invited them to the chancel. First I asked them to relax deeply. Then, while standing there in the chancel, I asked them to imagine the parents coming into the church, down the aisle and putting the baby in my arms. "Picture the baby cradled in my arms," I said. "Now come with me as we go to the altar." We went to the altar. "Put your hands on my shoulder." They did and I symbolically laid the baby on the altar, praying, "Infinite Father, we give this baby to thee who created her just as you created us all. Our love for her wants her to live. Our love for Thee wants your will to be done. She is yours. Amen." Sometime that night the baby ate and absorbed her food. She grew to be a fine little girl in our church.

Words? Invaluable! But words use only half of the brain God gave us, the left cerebral hemisphere. We leave out the part that houses inspiration, spatial vision and emotion.

"Let us pray **to** thee, dear Lord-not **about** thee. And let us use all our gifts: words, meditation, active listening, and visualizing. Thus may we come to know thee so personally and so constantly, that we need but tilt our hearts in thy direction to receive our vision. and our strength. Amen."

What's the Difference?

Some things are impossible to imagine; one of these is a world without difference. I always considered variation a thoughtful technique God used in creation to make life more interesting for us, his children. Like the automobile commercial says, "Wouldn't life be dull if all cars were the same color!"

Wouldn't life be dull if God had created only one kind of tree, one kind of dog, one kind of flower and, yes, one kind of human. It's a little frightening to think of every single person looking exactly as I look. God started right out with difference when creating people, as the Bible says: "male and female created he them." So Eve looks at Adam and says, "We're different."

"Oh," says Adam, "you noticed."

"Yeah," she says, "I've got more ribs than you."

I enjoy looking out my front window and watching people strolling on the beach. There are thin people, circumferentially challenged people, short people, tall people, young people, old people. And the couples are usually quite different—one tall, one short, one fair haired, one red-headed, etc. All of which indicates that we like difference in our mates as well as nature in general. And then, often, I muse about the sand, every grain different from every other, the gulls, the fish, the plant life in the sea—such an infinite variety and I'm led to say with the Psalmist: *O Lord, our Lord, how magnificent is thy name in all the earth.*

I thought of difference as a choice God made in creating the natural world. But I was startled out of my complacency by a statement made by the physicist, Frank Close, in his book: *Lucifer's Legacy: The Meaning of Asymmetry*. He writes: ". . . the creation of a perfectly symmetrical universe would have precluded there being any intelligent life, ever." What he is saying is that **God could not create life without a profusion of differences**. Existence is founded on difference. So when God dreamed of—as the Bible says—*making humankind in our own image,*" asymmetry and difference were an integral part of that Image. Why? Because difference is divine.

Let us think deeply, the next time we try to knead and twist our husband, wife, child, parent, worker, friend into our own image. We are working against God's plan for us. Even if we somehow succeed, the result could prove tragic. Difference is built in at the factory. Look at the following simple illustration.

A man buys a pedigreed dog. He wants his dog to win a prize at a dog show, so he takes it to a trainer who teaches the dog to hold it's tail just right, it's head just right and walk just right. Then he takes the dog to a dog barber who puffs the tail here the legs there till *his dog is a perfect image of every other dog in it's breed.* He has eradicated difference in some small degree. Finally he takes the dog to the annual dog show and what do you know, it wins the blue ribbon. Who wins the blue ribbon? The man wins the blue ribbon. He should wear it on his lapel—the dog couldn't care less.

If God loves "different," why are we so stuck on "same"? Every guy wants to have rippling abs and bulging biceps and every girl to look like a magazine cover girl. In Jesus' day the Pharisees were just like that dog owner. They knew exactly how every good Jew should eat, act with strangers, behave on the Sabbath and a thousand other things. They—and only they—knew exactly what God wanted each person to act like think like, look like and be like. It was these same Pharisees that Jesus was poking fun at when he ridiculed their regulations for cleanliness (straining a gnat) and condemned their lack of compassion (swallowing a camel).

I should, then, accept difference, appreciate difference, love difference, but I confess there are some things—different though they might be—that I cringe upon viewing. I'm going to lose any teenage readers here, but I have to be honest. A partial list: rings in nose, tongue and belly button, pants that two people could fit into, orange spiked hair, and music with no tune. If difference is beauty, I should be applauding these gems of deviation. But at least I don't ridicule. Isn't that a sign of Christian love? Instead of criticizing I put my hand over my mouth and mutter, "Only God could love that." I think I've got to do better, though if I'm going to make it to heaven. I've got to look at those "unfortunates" through God's eyes and with his help maybe I can inch forward.

I love the old gospel hymn "When we all get to heaven, what a day of rejoicing that will be!" But what if I arrive at the Pearly Gates, ring the bell, the door opens and there stands a tall, good-looking man with size fifty pants, a ring in his nose and spiked orange hair, and he says, "Good morning, Duane, I've been expecting you. I'm Jesus!"

Pardon me while I go out to find someone quite different from me to love.

God's Great Plus Sign

A family visited a famous cathedral. The small son stood in awe of the spaciousness and grandeur for a moment then said, "What's that big plus on the wall?"

Yes, what is that plus we see above the altar in church, on lapels and on chains around the neck? What does it mean? If you were wearing a cross and someone asked what the cross meant to you, how would you answer? It might not seem odd that our great plus sign has more than one meaning for ordinary church people, but does it not seem strange that the great leaders of the Christian Church have held differing views about the fundamental meaning of the cross? and that the meaning, according to church leaders, has changed through the years, but it has. First I'll outline briefly the three most prominent meanings that have held sway down through history. They are called the Triple AAAs, because they were given to the world by Augustine, Anselm, and Abelard. After I give you theirs I'll give you mine (what gall!).

According to Saint Augustine, the devil took humanity hostage by getting people to disobey God in the Garden of Eden. God said, *I want my children back. What are your demands? What must I pay to get them back?* And Satan answered, *Your son.* Finally God gave the devil what he asked, but in a way the devil could not expect. He offered Jesus to the devil on a cross. He caught the devil. The cross became a trap for Satan. In this sense Jesus died on the cross as a ransom for our sins. *For even the Son of Man did not come to be served, but to serve, and to give his life as a ransom for many.* [Mark 10:45]

Saint Anselm thought of the crucifixion, not as a ransom, but an atonement. This view emphasizes God's Justice. The mountain of sins accumulated by God's children demanded justice and so Jesus shed his blood so man wouldn't have to. It is called the Substitution Theory. Many of our great hymns involve this view: like *Jesus, keep me near the cross, there a precious fountain* by Fannie Crosby, and Isaac Watt's *Alas and did my Savior bleed? . . . . was it for sins that I have done?* In this view Jesus doesn't offer his life to the devil for our freedom; he offers his life to his Father for our freedom. Horace Bushnell, who did not like this view, called it the "slaughterhouse theory of atonement."

The third "A," promulgated by Abelard, is called the "Moral Influence Theory." He doesn't present the devil as an extortioner or think of God as an executioner, but rather of Jesus as teacher par excellence, and an example for living we can only strive to match. The death of Christ does not change God's attitude toward us or to our sins, but pictures, as the great hymn says: *The love of God is greater far than tongue or pen can ever tell; it goes beyond the highest star and reaches to the lowest hell.*

My personal interpretation of the great plus sign? In my college days I read a book, the name of which I forget, that defined Christianity in such a way that it gave me a mystical experience. The cross, it said, symbolizes two things. The upright piece is our personal and direct relationship with God while the cross piece is the arms of God, reaching out, embracing us and the world in love. And of course, God's arms are our arms. So the cross means to me my personal relationship with God through Jesus, and my love for others. There's no W in front of this theory but it is one that has stood the test of time for me and one I can explain to anyone who asks and which brings me great happiness and joy.

Maybe the little boy who mixed up his memory verse wasn't so far wrong at that. He reported to his mother what he had learned: *God so loved the world that he gave his only begotten Son, that whosoever believeth in him might not perish but have ever laughing life.*

Seeing In the Dark

Chuck Snow was a reporter for the Haverhill Gazette. He was one of those people who could talk on any subject with all kinds of people, was well read and did high quality reporting. Chuck Snow was blind.

I was sitting in on a meeting where he was in attendance as a reporter, taking notes with a tape recorder. But he was also listening to something on his radio through ear plugs. I said, "Chuck what's with the radio?" And he said, "I'm watching the ball game." He could "see" in the dark.

There are many kinds of darkness and many ways of dealing with it. Chuck's darkness was the inability of his visual organs to transmit physical light to his brain. But he created a visual field in his brain by using his other senses.

Sometimes our visual apparatus is OK but there is no physical light to be transmitted, as on a pitch black night. It was on such a night in Korea, 1951, that I went to the Fire Direction Center to have a cup of coffee and some conversation. One of the men asked me if I would like to go out to look at some night vision equipment they were setting up. What else to do? I went. The apparatus looked like a box the size of a large camera set on a tripod "Look where the scope is pointing," said one of the crew, "and tell me what you see." "I see blackness," I said, "night." "Now look through this scope." I did and was startled to see men in uniform (American) moving about and carrying equipment. The distance I was told was about two hundred yards, a good drive on a golf course. He tried to explain about infra red light, cathode ray tubes and phosphor screens, and I kept saying, "Uhuh," but I didn't really understand it—didn't really ***see*** his explanation. I was in the dark two ways: The dark of night and dark of unknowing.

We are born with this latter kind of darkness. A baby knows only a few things: when it is hungry, when it is in pain and when it is loved. Someone has defined a baby as *a small bundle with noise on one end and dirt on the other.* Watch a baby examining its hand. It is an interesting thing, this hand. When it moves out of sight, it is gone forever, and when it reappears in the baby's view it is a different hand, a new miracle. The same with the presence of the mother. When mother goes out of the room she is gone forever and when she returns she is another mother, a miracle. Then the baby learns it can make the hand disappear and return at will and does it over and over again. We know a light has gone on in the dark of unknowing. And then the baby learns it can bring the mother back with a forlorn wail. What power! Another light in the darkness.

Just so the great task of education goes on. And how sad in our world that so much mental darkness exists. Millions cannot read or write. We create mission schools and many learn to read, but it is a drop in the bucket—like trying to turn a lake pink by dropping a bit of dye into it.

One missionary, however, found a way to multiply the good a missionary can do. His name is Frank Laubach. He has been called the "Apostle to the Illiterates," the "foremost teacher of our times," and the tribes of the Belgian Congo called him Okombekombe, which means "mender of broken baskets." His method is called "Each One Teach One." A contract is made: *I'll teach you if you promise to teach at least one other person.* Teach them to read and give them a Bible. What better way to turn on the light, the Light of the World, in that dark continent.

Another form of darkness is despondency. To be despondent is to see life painted in black and to see no way out. Many things in life can cause us to be despondent. One is the loss of a precious relationship. George Matheson, Scottish Presbyterian minister and hymn writer, planned to be married but his fiancee broke off the engagement almost on the wedding day. She canceled out because Matheson was blind and she didn't think she could live with that. And though he was blind, and having been let go by one love, he wrote about another love that would never let him go:

> *O love that will not let me go, I rest my weary soul in thee . . . a joy that seekest me through pain. I trace the rainbow through the rain and feel the promise is not vain that morn shall tearless be.*

Then there's the darkness about the meaning of life, about whether we are on the right road. Bunyan's Pilgrim felt the forward pull of his journey. He hoped he was making progress toward the gate to heaven though he could not see it. When he spoke to an evangelist about it, he was asked, "Do you see yonder wicket gate?" He answered no. "Do you see yonder shining light?" He said he thought he did. Then said the Evangelist, "Keep that light in your eye, and go directly thereto, so shalt thou then see the Gate." Keep that light in your eye, the Light of the World, and go straight ahead. So shall you find the Gate of Heaven.

Sometimes like Pilgrim, I, as a pastor, find the light ahead getting dim, yet I am constrained to point out the Light of the World to others. Once when a twenty-four-year-old mother died of cancer, I was groping in the dark for answers. Why would God let this happen, leaving a husband and two little ones to go on alone? I dreaded the house call I had to make. How would I explain to Laura, six, and Bobbie, four? I walked into their living room and had barely sat down when Laura ran over to me and said, "Mommy's all better now. She is in Heaven with Jesus."

A floodlight went on in my heart. "Lo, I am with you always," I heard him say, and I could see in the dark again. After all, he **is** the light of the world.

The Little Foxes

We often think it is the man-eating tigers of life that "spoil the vine," do us in, trip us up, bring us low. I contend, however, that people seem to come to grips with these extraordinary setbacks of life better than they do the "little foxes," the almost imperceptible ongoing negatives of existence.

What are the man-eating tigers? A death in the family, terminal cancer, stroke, divorce, loss of job, etc. And the little foxes? Worry, fear, gossip, suspicion, the daily grind. Amos, of the Amos and Andy radio show, put it so well: "Andy, you know what the biggest trouble with livin' is?"

"No, Amos, what?"

"The trouble is that life is so daily!"

We sometimes call it the daily grind. I think Charlie Brown grasped the idea. He and Linus were walking home from when Linus asked, "Why do we have to go to school, anyway?" We have to go to school," said Charlie Brown so we can get good grades and graduate and then go to high school, so we can get good grades and graduate so we can go to college and get good grades and graduate so we can get a good job and make enough money so we can pay to send our kids to school so they can . . . ."

The underlying meaning of what Amos and Charlie Brown are talking about has to do with stress. Life is so daily. Worry and fear, two of the little foxes are so daily. If we don't deal with the stress, it becomes distress. Distress not only ruins the grapes on the vine, it destroys the vine itself. Our emotional stability itself is in danger. The unrealistic behavior we sometimes see people engage in can be in response to their loss of emotional balance. Perhaps like the man in the next paragraph.

He was riding on the train, tearing up bits of paper and throwing them out the window. Another passenger asked, "What are you doing?"

"I'm scaring away the tigers."

"There are no tigers around here!"

"See, it works."

Here is a modern parable that sheds some light on the meaning of "life is so daily" and "little foxes spoil the vines." Automobiles are made to withstand some pretty severe bumps. What they cannot stand, however, is constant vibration. A car can be in an accident and be made as good as new again, but the hourly, daily, constant vibrations create metal fatigue which will eventually send the car to the automobile graveyard.

Stress is the vibrations in our lives and—one way or another—we will handle these little foxes. The question is, will the result be good for us or bad. One little fox that vibrates in people's lives is worry. Worrying is putting a question mark where God wishes to put a period. Worry begins as concern and then gets lost. Being concerned is a natural mental function. When we are concerned about a life event, we should do what we can about the situation then put it in God's hands. As John Wesley once said, "Work as though everything depended on you and then pray as though everything depended on God." No question mark just a period.

A doctor told his patient he would have to stop worrying, but the patient said, "I can't do that, Doc; I have to keep on worrying."

"Why?"

"Because the things I worry about never happen."

Wouldn't it be nice if things worked that way! It might help to think about the following: Susan Stiles, of Foley, Minnesota, has two little girls ages 4 and 6. As she tucks them into bed each night, she recites the following: "Remember, you are special to God and remember also how much we love you. Sleep loose."

She wants her children to relax and let go into the love of God that surrounds each of them.

What a much better way to not only sleep but to live life, not sleep tight, live tight (with stress) but live in the arms of God. Paul was advising his friends at Corinth (and us) to live this way when he ended his letter to them (I Cor 13:11): *Now brothers, goodbye! . . . live in peace, and God, the source of love and peace will be with you.*

Live loose.

Who Wants to Be a Millionaire?

Little Tommy was reading when he came upon a word that stumped him. He asked his father, "Dad, what's a millionaire?" The father I answered, "A millionaire is a person who has three million dollars."

"Oh," Tommy answered, "I guess I am a oneaire."

Tommy has given us a way to rate our personal wealth. Subtract your liabilities from your assets and add aire to the answer. We could end up a tenaire, a hundredaire or even a thousandaire. We could, of course, end up being a minusaire.

Who wants to be a millionaire, anyway? According to the bestseller *The Millionaire Next Door* 2800 people in the US wanted to be. That's the number of first-generation millionaires there were at the time of writing. And they became such without magic, luck or lottery. They saved, budgeted, lived frugally and bit the bullet. They didn't have expensive cars, clothes, homes or live ostentatiously. They just had a million dollars in the bank. As far as anyone could tell, they were the person next door.

If you or I had a million dollars in the bank, would it change us? Would we go on a buying spree? If we did and bought an expensive home and an expensive car there would just be enough for our kids' education. So who wants it? Most people you ask would say, "You bet I'd like to have a million Dollars!"

Why? All we can buy with money is stuff—things. Money can't buy friends, though it might get us a better class of enemies. And on the plus side, it would sure keep us in touch with our kids. Common wisdom has it that money can't buy happiness, but some wag pontificated, "That just shows they don't know where to shop."

When I was in my first parish I had one preaching suit and a car that kept breaking down. If someone had offered me a million dollars free and clear at that time, would I have taken it? I, like George, cannot tell a lie. I would have. Would it have changed me? Probably. Would I have made the same choices and followed the same path? Probably not. For these reasons I am devoutly glad that an easy road was not offered me. I would not take a million dollars for the sweat, the tears, the hard times, the difficult choices, the dangerous incidents that were a part of my lot. I kid you not! I look at the furrow I have plowed and am flooded with gratitude. Maybe, if I had a million dollars, things would have been pretty much the same, but I wouldn't want to chance it. I had to work for what I have, and I love work. I wouldn't want to be like the man who discovered a machine that would do half his work, so he went out and bought two of them.

I Think Mr. Ecclesiastes (9: 10) had it right when he wrote *Whatsoever your hand finds to do, do it with your might; for there is no work or substance, or knowledge or wisdom, in the grave where you are going.* He didn't mention heaven; I hope there is work to do up there. I would go mad just sitting on a pink cloud for a thousand years.

Work is a blessing and important to our well-being. Consider the dream one man had. He dreamed he inherited a million dollars. He got ready to go down town, get the money and transfer it to his account. He got in the shower and it wouldn't work. He tried to shave but the shaver wouldn't shave. He tried to make a cup of coffee but the coffee-maker wouldn't perk. The toaster wouldn't toast. He went out to get a paper but they hadn't been delivered. He waited for a bus but it never came. He asked a passer-by what was going on and he said, "Haven't you heard? Everyone was given a million dollars and no one is working." Life came to a standstill.

In general this fits well with the spirit of Jesus and the warnings of the Apostle. Paul writes to Timothy (6:10) *The love of money is the root of all evil.* Neither Paul nor Jesus condemned riches—only the love of wealth and overweening desire to be rich. There is no evil to which such motives cannot lead.

As far as I can remember, I've never preached a sermon against the love for and the accumulation of wealth. Maybe it never seemed necessary in the congregations I pastored, or is that rationalization. Martin Luther preached such sermons. With great fervor he thundered, "He who has enough to satisfy his wants, and nevertheless ceaselessly labors to acquire riches, either to acquire a higher social position, or live without labor, or that his sons may become men of wealth and importance, is incited by a damnable avarice, sensuality and pride." He went even further in denunciation of usury or putting out one's money in order to gain interest. "The greatest misfortune of the German nation is easily the traffic in interest. It was invented by the devil." And he refused to administer the sacraments to them or give them absolution or even a Christian burial.

A far cry from today when preachers are declaiming that God wants us to have good homes, cars and the things money can buy. "It's a sign of his favor," they cry. Martin must be turning over in his grave.

Looking at this change between the sixteenth century and today, wealth seems to be a relative matter—if you come into a fortune you suddenly gain relatives. Just kidding. I mean that we always have more wealth than some people and less wealth than others. Like the man who started going to communist party meetings and was going to join the party till one day he quit cold. Asked why, he said, "At the last meeting they said that if all the wealth in the US were divided equally, everyone would have $2,000." So, why did you quit? "Because," he said, "I have $5,000."

Million—schmillion. I wouldn't trade places with anyone in the world. Would you?

The Family Tree

A Beacon Hill dowager in Boston noticed that all her friends had a family tree in a fancy book, prominently displayed in their homes. She wanted such a book to display so as to be on a social par with the rest of the elite. She called a genealogist, gave him as many names as she could think of and commissioned him to bring back a book like her rich neighbors had. He came back a week later and said, "I've run into a problem." She said, "Yes, I know. It's Uncle Henry. He committed murder and died in the electric chair in Sing Sing. But you know how to fix such things. Do the best you can." He was gone for six months. When he came back he handed her a beautifully bound genealogy of her family. She took it and quickly thumbed through the pages to the entry for "Uncle Henry." It read: *Uncle Henry: he occupied the chair of applied electricity in a great upper state institution. He was an indefatigable worker, in fact he was in harness to the very end. His passing came as a great shock.*

Like the dowager, most people will find a black sheep or a skeleton in the closet if they go back enough generations. Still there's a fascination about knowing who one's ancestors were. Polly and I have travelled far and wide seeking information about our great-great-greats, even as far as Holland where I walked the ancient brick streets of Delfzijl my grandmother walked as a girl; and I stood on the dikes and looked out on the North Sea as she must have done many a time.

Neither of us found royalty in our blood line, though Polly had a Scottish ancestor, one of the founders of Buckfield, Maine, who had been in the employ of King James the First and Queen Elizabeth. But the question that calls for an answer is: "Why do people want to know? What difference can it make? Even children who are adopted and raised by loving people have a need to find out who their "real" parents were. The answer, I think, lies in the genetic stuff we are made of.

The word *gene* comes from the same root as *genealogy and generation*. So genealogy is the study of generations. Some biophysicists claim that entelechy—a road map of the future—is built into every gene. This map must be in the mind of God, a general, over-all goal toward which all life is struggling. Someone has said, "How can we know where we are going if we don't know where we have been?" Maybe we're seeking a glimpse of the future by searching the past, studying our genealogy. That's not for me. I chart my ancestors because It's fun. But that begs the question. I still don't know *why* it's fun. I think I'll let the "why" go and agree with Abraham Lincoln who said, "I can't do much about who my ancestors were, but I can do something about what kind of an ancestor I'm becoming."

Unlike Lincoln, the Israelites held blood relationships to be of utmost importance. It validated their name. Their name was all important. It was as if they didn't exist unless their name was in the genealogical chart. Jesus, on the other hand was like Abe Lincoln, he seemed not to be interested in his lineage, though I'm sure Jesus knew all the "begats" in Jewish history. But he was an existentialist, perhaps the first one. He spoke about now, today, and the Kingdom of God being **here**. He had no need to look back in his history to gain strength for his future. "God's Kingdom is among you," he said. It has arrived. "All you need to do is step into it." *The Spirit of the Lord is upon me*, he said to his home town congregation . . . . *To proclaim the year of the Lord . . . . Today this scripture has been fulfilled in your hearing*. For those words they drove him out of town and wanted to throw him over a cliff. This was a message the Jewish hierarchy didn't want to hear so they killed him. But thanks to Jesus, we know we are already in the Kingdom and therefore experience fellowship with the King.

So I will continue to be grateful for the constant presence of God and the knowledge that I don't have to own a pedigree to avail myself of it. And along with millions of others I will continue my hobby, fully assured by now that my ancestors were all simple, down-to-earth people. In a way I am thankful that I don't find the rich and the famous there. It might make me "uppity" like one member of the DAR who stopped at Sammy Shapiro's shop to get a newspaper. Sammy, being an affable fellow, tried to engage her in conversation. He asked her how she was, how her family was, did she think it would rain, etc. She would have none of it. She put her nose in the air as if to say, "Who are you to speak to me!" But Sammy continued, so she cut him short with, "I'll have you know, my good man, that my ancestors came over on the Mayflower!"

Still in his cheerful way Sammy said, "I'll have you know that **my** ancestors crossed the Red Sea on foot!"

Rah-rah for Sammy! I'd rather have him in my family tree than her, any day!

Irritations

Al Capp, in his Dogpatch family, had Daisy Mae cutting 'Lil Abner's hair while he was reading the morning news. "It says here," Abner read, "that according to U.S. Govamint statistics, one half of all marriages will end in divorce." Pappy, sitting in an iron tub getting scrubbed by Mammy, says, "Then one of us has got to git a divorce cause I believe in U.S. Govamint statistics."

One wag opined: "The greatest cause of divorce in this country is statistics." Apparently Pappy and Mammy Yokum agree, though the dynamite underlying statistics is (among other things) irritation. Seems like we can't stand irritation today like we did in yesteryear. Listen to one woman discussing with another her approaching divorce.

"My husband is impossible! He irritates me so much I'm even losing weight."

"Why don't you leave him?" asked a friend.

"I'm going to as soon as I lose fourteen more pounds."

Irritations go with the territory. I have yet to meet a husband or wife who doesn't encounter spousal irritation once in a while (present company excepted, of course). In fact, irritation is a part of the total definition of animal cellular life. When irritability is gone life is gone. And besides, the marriage ceremony doesn't say, "Till irritability do us part." It says, "Till *debts* do us part." Maybe it's the same thing.

So, besides debts, what other irritations cause marriages to come unglued? Eating crackers in bed? Snoring? Using the sports page to wrap the garbage in? Squeezing the middle of the toothpaste tube? Leaving the toilet seat up? Bringing unexpected guests for supper? Taking an inordinately long time to get ready to go out? It has been said: *If there are no differences in a marriage, there must be a lot of indifference.* Translated: *If there are no irritations in the marriage, there is little life left in the marriage.*

But marriages are not simply dead or alive; there are many gradations of "life" therein. One author rates them as "Angelic Twins," "Spare Time Battlers" and "Paranoid Predators." I haven't met the first and last types but in my first parish I got to know the middle type. I was making calls and came to the home of a couple in their sixties, pretty old, I thought at the time. We sat in the living room chatting, when the wife suddenly arose and left the room. I thought she had gone to get tea and cookies, which was fine with me, but she didn't come back. I didn't know what to say but finally decided on: "Did I say something?" "No," the husband said, "I did." He explained that they discovered early on that they both had hot tempers and that it got them in trouble a lot. They made an agreement. When either one felt the temperature rising he or she would leave the scene and cool off. "Really works," he said. "Been married over forty years! Sorry it happened when you were here. But she'll be back in a minute."

Now I'm older than they were then and I have encountered many different ways to handle irritation. Let me give you a few. The *I'm O.K.—You're O.K.* school advises us to learn to recognize the "glitch in the gut" and determine not to get hooked in a rising spiral of aggravation. Instead, we are to either 1) calmly ask a question to clarify the source of the grievance or 2) calmly make a statement about the subject that caused the irritation. Then there's the *Pull Your Own Strings* school which advises "getting *out* your feelings." Let 'em know who you are and how you feel. If you're angry, say so. Happy? Say so. Take charge of your feelings. Or the advice I give my students: keep an "Irritation Journal." At the end of the day write down each incident in which you were irritated and then describe what you said and/or did. Over a period of time some insights occur which help you to deal with irritations in constructive ways.

The book *The Relaxation Response* by Herbert Benson teaches us to respond to any sudden rise of adrenaline in our system, in marriage or out, with relaxation. No matter what the problem is, he says, we are better able to cope while relaxed. And we can get relaxed through physical activity We can hit the punching bag, jog, go out to the driving range and every time we hit the ball say, "Take this, (name deleted), and this and this."

Well, by now you get the idea that we don't have to obey the U.S. Govamint's statistics. There are ways to cope. The humorist, Seth Parker. wrote a piece about coping strategy. It was called *Staying Married*. "Yep," he says, "for fifty years now we've lived together, and we've never had an argument. I'm going to tell you the secret, and I'm not going to charge a thing for it. *A couple of evenings after we were married, Jane and me set down and had a good long talk. We realized that we had a good many years to make a go of it together, and we wanted some sort of plan to work on. We came to the followin' conclusion. We'd both have our own territory. It would be up to Jane to make all of the little decisions of life—the decisions about the house, and how much we'd give to the Church, and how the children would dress and like that. And that I would make all the big decisions, the vital decisions of life—those decisions that would affect our whole future.*"

"What about those big decisions?" says I.

"Oh," says he, "there ain't been no big decisions yet."

So, Mammy and Pappy Yokum, try one or two of these little coping strategies. If they work, you might even change the U.S Govamint statistics.

Boning Up On Bone

A regular reader of these letters asked me if I knew where the expression *to bone up on* came from. We both knew that *to bone up on* means to *learn more about*. But we didn't know what the word *bone* had to do with it. I had to find out. The answer was simple but buried in history. The expression originated in the middle of the last century with students "Bohning up for exams." Henry George Bohn published what was called a "guinea catalog" of classic works in literature and the sciences. Each classic was condensed, somewhat like the cliff notes of today. So if a student was behind in his reading and faced with an exam, he would grab Henry George's condensed classics and Bohn up.

But I could not stop there. What about "pulling a boner?" This is a twist on a baseball phrase "bonehead play," that came into use around 1900. All skulls are made of bone, but the theory was that men had different sized brains depending on how thick the skull was. Small brain thick skull and vice versa. Thus the epithet for some players: bonehead. Baseball errors were made by boneheads and were called "boners." In reality, any error ***we*** make is a mistake in judgment; any error someone else makes is a "boner."

Then, of course, there is "bone of contention" leading to "I have a bone to pick with you." This cliche is pretty visual and needs little interpretation. We simply have to visualize two dogs gnawing and pulling on the same bone. There is a little saving grace here—there is something social about it. It takes two to tango. One dog can't pick a bone with himself.

God had a bone to pick with Adam. When he told Adam he was going to perform major surgery on his rib cage to create a mate, someone to be with, to talk with and walk with. "You know," God said, "companionship."

Adam said, "Couldn't you take maybe a fingernail instead of a rib and make her a little less companionable?"

Imagine that! Right at the beginning! A bone of contention in the Garden of Eden.

If you started to read this letter without a drink in hand, you are probably "bone dry" by now. So am I. Lets both of us pause to get refreshed (moisturized) before we continue.

We have to keep moisturized, "make no bones about it." You back? O.K., me too. Had enough about bone cliches? Now you know why some people are leery of asking their preacher a question—especially if his nickname is "Windy." He might be something like the mother in the following story.

A little boy came home from school with a query. "Mom, where did I come from?" Getting nervous, she thought "I knew I had to tell him about the birds and bees sometime; guess this is it!" She had him sit beside her on the sofa while she spent a half hour telling her son the facts of life. The boy got tired of this. "I know all that stuff," he said "but Jimmy's from Boston and I wanna tell him where I come from". So much for idiomatic speech.

When we use the word "bone" as a cliche, there is no thought of actual bones, but if we have leukemia, the word "bone" takes on a whole new literal meaning. The marrow in the center of the bone, the "blood factory," begins to produce so many white bells that they crowd out the red cells, bringing about an illness that is fatal unless a marrow transplant can be arranged. A bone is no longer a cliche, but very real!

From antiquity, in almost every culture, one's skeleton was more than just bones it had mysterious powers. The bones of a martyr were possessions prized by individuals and churches. They were thought to have a miracle working potential. In the early days of the Israelites a dead person's bones were thought to retain healing powers. Some time following the death and burial of Elisha, a tomb was being prepared for another man. An enemy army was rumored to be approaching, so the burial party hastily opened Elisha's grave and thrust the corpse in. As soon as the body touched the bones of Elisha it was restored to life. A miracle! It seemed like soul and skeleton were synonymous.

When Isaiah prophesied *and God will guide you and make fat your bones,* he was saying, *God will invigorate you and strengthen the very core of your being.* Read Ezekiel's vision of the valley of the dry bones [37:1-14]. Put your critical mind in neutral and your intuitive mind in high gear. Visualize the bones of those slain by the enemies of Israel, literally covering this lower Tigris Euphrates valley. As God speaks through Ezekiel watch the bones come to life . . . bone to bone, bone to tendon, tendon to skin, and then God does CPR. Listen to the praises! Listen to the Haleluia Chorus! This is what God promises you and me when our spirits are bone dry—when we are too weary to go on. *I will invigorate you and strengthen your soul.* God will do his part if we do ours: trust—let go—let be—let God. Then we, too, as the old spiritual says, can be put back together again, "foot bone connected to the shin bone, shin bone connected to the leg bone, leg bone connected to the knee bone, knee bone connected to the hip bone . . . brain bone connected to the faith bone . . . all in the name of the Lord."

Certification

When I was a boy, living on the farm, we occasionally had a "trusty" from the nearby insane asylum working for us. His name was "Crazy John." John would chop wood, weed the garden, carry water, and that sort of thing. He had a pet crow that stayed with him, sometimes sitting on his shoulder. He would talk to the crow and the crow would chatter back. Crazy John said the crow could talk, but it didn't sound like real words to me. Crazy John said that he had to put a slit in the crows tongue to enable it to talk, that anybody could do that to a crow and make it talk. He even showed me the pocket knife with which this miraculous surgery was performed. He might have been crazy but he was a genius to me. Many years after I had left the farm I heard that Crazy John fell off a hay wagon and broke his neck while working for some farmer. I grieved a bit then. I liked Crazy John.

Crazy John was certified. I don't hear that word applied to the mentally ill now-a-days, though it is still in the dictionary. It meant he was insane and had the papers to prove it. I've known some people who were crazier than Crazy John who were never certified. What does it mean to "be certified?" We have certified public accountants, certified bills of sale, physicians certified as obstetricians, certified checks, certified mail and even certified milk.

Certified evolved from the Latin *certusfacere* (to make certain). That is why we hang our certificates on the wall. We are claiming "I am this or that not by my say-so but by experts who attest to it." Why do we need certification anyway? Because, sadly enough, we often look on others with a certain amount of reservation—even suspicion. Like the Quaker woman who said to her husband, "I think the whole world is daft except thee and me, and sometimes I wonder about thee."

Even churches are suspicious of the authenticity of other churches. A former member of an Episcopalian church asked to be a member of our Congregational church. We wrote to the Episcopalian church asking for a transfer of membership for this person. We got no response. Later, the pastor of that church admitted, with some embarrassment, "We don't believe the Congregational Church is a legitimate church. He explained. It had to do with apostolic succession—Jesus putting his hands on the head of Peter who put his hands on the head of a candidate for ordination, who afterward put his hands on the head of another candidate for ordination in succession all the way down to the present. A lay preacher (unordained) broke away from the Church of England and started the Congregational denomination. He was uncertified and that break in the apostolic succession made all succeeding Congregational ministers uncertified. No real transfer of membership could take place.

I wonder what Jesus would say about all this. I wonder if, when we reach the Golden Gates, there will be a mail slot to one side of the gate with the words above it "Place certificates here." No, when he said, *You must become as a little child to enter the kingdom of heaven* there was no *and be sure to get your certification.*

It is amazing what clergy and denominations have done because they believed it was the only way God would approve of it being done. Reminds me of the two men on a ward in the mental hospital talking. One with his hand in his vest stated, "I'm Napoleon."

"Yeah?" said another certified inmate, "who told you?" "God did."

Just then a voice from another room said, "I did not!"

But why should it be only the clergy who must become certified? Why should lay-people escape? Should not all Christians be certified? Instead of "Brother, are you saved?" it would be, "Brother, are you certified?" Naw, it's hard enough to be a real Christian without worrying about being board certified and having a proper license.

Real Christianity **is** hard wrote M. Scott Peck in his book *Further Along the Road Less Traveled.* He said, "If the clergy preached the real truth of the Gospels, their congregations would flee out the door." And someone else has said, "Christianity has not been tried and found hard; it has been found hard and not tried."

Not so for all Jesus' followers. One teenage girl was left with two younger siblings after their parents were killed in a car accident. She decided to bring up her brother and sister herself. She cleaned houses, scrubbed floors and did laundry, to make enough to keep the family together. She saw that her brother and sister got to Sunday School, but never got there herself—always working. Her hands got calloused and hard. Some do-gooders from the church took her to task for not coming to Sunday School. "What will you tell the angels when they ask you why you were not in church?"

She said, "I'll just show them my hands."

She's certified.

Something Other Than You Are

It has been said that the doctrine of karma—transmigration and rebirth—is so logical that if two-thirds of the earth's population did not already believe it, it would be hailed by westerners today as a major philosophical breakthrough. Before recorded history, when writing was in hieroglyphics, reincarnation was the accepted explanation of life and death. In the Hindu "Bible," the Bhagavad-Gita, we read the beautiful words, echoed by the Apostle Paul *As a man, casting off worn out garments, takes on new ones, so the dweller in the body, casting off worn out bodies, enters into others that are new.* And six hundred years before Jesus, Gautama Buddha said: *There is no escaping the result of man's actions; without the cycle of rebirth life is meaningless and without purpose.* The chief goal of living was, according to Buddha, to live so purely that one could "get off the wheel"and not have to reenter this vale of tears. The Essenes—forerunners of John the Baptist and Jesus—believed fully in reincarnation and early Christians held the belief as a matter of course. St. Augustine wrote in his confessions: *Did I not live in another body before entering my mother's womb?*

Reincarnation is not my personal explanation of life and death, but it is a fascinating concept and I get into some interesting conversations on the subject with students in my Death and Dying class. It cannot be proved or disproved, just as God cannot be proved or disproved, because we have not been given the mental ability to pierce the veil and see the beyond and the past, no matter what Shirley MacLaine says.

One of my favorite books is *Archy and Mehitabel.* Archy is a poet and philosopher who died and was reincarnated into the body of a cockroach. Mehitabel, the cat, was the reincarnation of the regal Cleopatra of the Nile. Archy, a strict moralist, provides many insights on what is wrong with American life. Mehitabel, without morals, or so Archy thinks, enjoys life to the full, singing her refrain over and over, "Toujours gai, toujours gai, there's still a dance in the old dame yet." She was once keeping company with a coyote but swore that nothing sexual happened between them, but Archy wonders, since her new baby cats go yip, yip, yip instead of meaow. Archy preaches to her but with little effect.

How does a cockroach manage to write? He was crawling around in a newspaper office one night, picking up a crumb from somebody's lunch here and a bit of editing paste there when he found himself on the top of a typewriter. Something of the poet stirred in his cockroach breast. One can only believe that it was divine inspiration that caused him to leap from the top of that typewriter and land on his head on one of the keys. He heard the click, crawled up and saw a letter on the paper in the typewriter and his life was forever changed! After many headaches and laborious climbing and jumping he was able to leave notes to the owner of the typewriter, Don Marquis, columnist for the Chicago Sun. Don Marquis began to copy some of these into his daily column and Archy's fame was assured. His bits of wisdom are a little hard to read since he couldn't press two keys at once, making punctuation difficult, but with a little effort his offerings can be deciphered. And they are worth the effort. In the following bit Archy is complaining about reincarnation.

> well boss here i am a cockroach still boss i am disgusted with death and transmigration i would rather not inhabit any body at all than inhabit a cockroaches body but it seems that it is my destiny my doom my punishment when the copy boy swatted me the other night i died my first sensation was one of glad relief what body will the soul of archy transmigrate into now i asked myself will i go higher in the scale of life and inhabit the body of a butterfly or a dog or will i sink lower and go into the carcass of a spider or a politician i sat on a blade of grass and waited and wondered what it would be i hoped it wouldn't be anything too soon it was kind of nice being nothing and feel my soul flutter in the breeze well while i was sitting there thinking i had a swooning sensation and when i came to i was in the flesh again dad gum it i lifted first one leg and then another to see what i was this time and imagine my chagrin when i found myself inside another cockroach the exact counterpart of the one that was smashed whats the use of dying if it dont get you anywhere so i suppose i was not good enough to be promoted and not bad enough to be set back boss a thing like that makes a fellow feel awful humble say boss i wish you would sprinkle a little cereal in the bottom of the waste paper basket archy

The trouble with the theory of transmigration, as far as I can see, is that it allows little room for love as a motivation. Reincarnation provides us with an incentive (like struggling up the corporate ladder for more money and prestige) but says little about the quality of our relationships. The Gospel of love (compassion and empathy), on the other hand, says if we help each other we all rise together. Here's an old illustration of the difference between the concepts.

A man died and awoke in the other world. He saw everyone sitting at banquet tables loaded with every luscious food and drink imaginable. He thought he was in heaven till he realized that every person's arms were stiff as boards. Every one was trying to flip bits of the delicious food into his mouth, missing, and groaning in messy misery. "I must be in hell," he thought, and begged to be transferred to heaven. He was whisked away and found himself in an identical situation with tables, luscious food, and even stiff armed diners. He was about to complain to his guides when he noticed that each person was picking up food with his stiff arm and feeding a neighbor.

So even if we decide to believe in Karma, perhaps the best way to get off the wheel is to love our neighbor.

Tribulation

Said the mistress to her maid one morning, "Clara, you look like you've lost your best friend. Cheer up! Put on a smile! Things will begin to look better."

"No maam, I can't do that," said Clara.

"Why not?"

"Cause the Lord sent me a tribulation and he expects me to tribulate so that's what I'm going to do."

I can't believe that God sends tribulations. The word originally meant pounding corn into meal using a heavy sledge. The old idea that God "tries us in the refiner's fire" simply does not jive with Jesus' picture of the loving father. *If a son asks his father for bread, will he give him a stone? If he asks for a fish, will he give him a snake?* said Jesus. He is saying to us, "Your heavenly father will stand in relationship to you as you stand in relationship to your child."

Think. Would you put your child through a drug habit, a divorce, a loss of job, etc., just to strengthen character? The more realistic and meaningful picture of our God is of the father or mother who stands with the child in all its troubles to encourage, help and guide.

Tribulations will come; that's for sure and they will pass and that's for sure. And if we love God, our father, he will be helping us to stand firm "till the cloud passes by." I think that's why he had Paul write that great verse to us: *We know that in all things God works for good with those who love him.* As I've said in another place, "We should pray not, *Why have you got it in for me, God?* but *What have you got in this for me?*

I like one of Walt Whitman's lines that reflects this: "Have you not learned from those who disputed the passage with you?"

Steven disputed the passage with Paul. Steven was one of those new radicals called Christians. Paul was a fire-breathing, militaristic agent of the establishment; he was rooting out and killing all who followed Jesus. As he stood on the edge of that gravel pit and watched Steven's life ground out under the hurled stones, did Paul feel victorious? I think not. Steven was praying for him. Oh what Paul learned that day!

One of the sorest tribulations in my own life was being betrayed by a friend. Every time I met the one who had been a friend there was a gulf between us. The greatest tribulation in my life was the death of my son. Grief itself is tribulation. How best to deal with it? I came across the definition of prayer as a loving conference with God. Why not make it a loving three-member committee meeting? As relaxed as I can get—oftentimes in bed—God, the other person and I sit conversing and listening. Insights, idea and peace result from these sessions. Some who face tribulation, who find their passage disputed, become vengeful. Others become self-pitying, but those who learn from tribulation build character. As the roots of a tree sink deeper with every storm, so the fibre of our faith is strengthened by adversity—if we love God and are willing to grow.

A small boy's mother said, "I spank you because I love you." The boy's reply was, "Please don't love me so much!"

If we tribulate and think it's God's hand spanking us, let's turn over, take hold of the spanking-hand, stand up and grow.

Gurus of Sin

Bob Thaves, in his comic strip, FRANK & ERNEST, has Frank and Ernie leaving church conversing with one another. Frank is saying to Ernest, "Has it ever occurred to you that the pastor knows an awful lot about sin?"

Well, I resemble Frank's remark. I know a lot about sin. And it's all legitimate! I studied about it in seminary, I counseled erring church members and I watch soap operas (for educational purposes, of course). I'm not sure whether I know as much about sin as one preacher. He advertised Sunday's sermon title in the newspaper: **128 Sins Humans Commit**. He was flooded with mail requesting a copy of the list. Apparently there were people who wanted to find out what sins they were missing.

I resemble the cartoon in another way. The pastor of the church I grew up in was also an expert on sin. At least he mentioned it many times in his sermons. Actually, if he preached a sermon *without* using the word sin, the congregation would think the preacher was slipping. Looking back from my perch on a pile of years, I believe those preachers, all unwittingly, I'm sure, were child abusers—they caused us children more psychic pain than can be measured. Listen to this piece of a sermon I have indelibly branded on my memory. *My friends, I was conducting a funeral for a man who had sinned against God's law. How do I know that? Because, right in the middle of the funeral service the corpse sat bolt upright and in a most unearthly voice said, "Please—**Please**—PLEASE! Just a little bit of water; just a cup of water! It's so hot down here!* I probably didn't sleep much that night. I was ever worried about whether or not this action or that behavior of mine could be classified as a sin. If I said "damn," I sinned. If I engaged in a game using playing cards, I sinned; If I got angry with my mother, I sinned; and, as the King of Siam said, "Etceter-ah, etceter-ah, etceter-ah."

And please, gentle reader, don't mistake my concerns as mere childish conduct. My fear of going to hell was extremely real. No day ended without my kneeling at bedtime, recounting what sins I could remember, asking for mercy and then adding, "And forgive me for the sins I committed but can't remember."

Which makes me wonder—does God hold us accountable for sins we forgot we even committed? There are such sins. Psychiatrist's couches are filled with people who feel a terrible sense of guilt but don't know what for. And the doctors charge a fortune to do what God will do for free. It's called Salvation. What a bargain!

Philosophers deal with it by calling it "existential guilt," The guilt we have just for being human—just for being related to Adam—just because Adam and Eve decided to add fruit to their diet.

Children knew this as early, at least, as 1691 when in school they read in their **New England Primer**: *In Adam's fall We sinned all. / Young Obadias, David, Josias, All were pious*, Etc.

Now I hear you asking, "OK Sacred Agent 007, enough about generalities. What sins did you commit in your boyhood on the farm?" And I really would like to satisfy your curiosity, but you see, it all depends on how you define "sin."

The dictionary says sin is an offense against the moral law or a transgression against the laws of God. The Bible says *Anyone, then, who knows the good he ought to do and doesn't do it, sins.* [In which case most of us sin most of the time] *What causes fights and quarrels among you? Don't they come from your desires that battle within you? You want something but don't get it. You kill and covet, but you cannot have what you want. You quarrel and fight . . . you spend what you get on your pleasures.* [Sounds right up to date, doesn't it? This is James, the brother of Jesus, speaking (4:1-17) He goes on] . . . . *Submit yourselves to God, resist the devil, and he will flee from you. Come near to God, you sinners, and he will come near to you. Purify your hearts . . . do not slander one another.* And John, the beloved disciple, gives this advice: *If we confess our sins, he is faithful and just and will forgive us our sins.* [I John 1:8-9]

And this is echoed in the petition that millions make every Sunday morning when they open the Book of Common Prayer and say together the General Confession . . . *We have strayed from thy ways like lost sheep. We have offended against thy holy laws. We have left undone those things we ought to have done and we have done those things we ought not to have done* . . . which sounds a lot like the words of the Apostle Paul: *For the good that I would do I do not; but the evil which I would not, that I do.* [Romans 8:19]

Paul is talking about sins of **commission** and sins of **omission**. A Sunday School teacher asked her class about sins of omission and Jane answered: "Those are the sins we should have committed and didn't."

Excuse this guru of sin while he goes to pick out a sin or two from the list in preparation for his next sermon.

There are Two Kinds of People . . .

. . . those who say there are two kinds of people and those who don't. I'm one of the former. I say there is one kind of person who will find something to find fault about in the best of times and another kind who will find something to be thankful for in the worst of times, like the woman coming out of anesthesia at her dentist's. The doctor said, "I had to remove all your teeth except two."

She wiggled her gums and said, "Thank the Lord!"

Why are you thanking the Lord when you've just lost all but two of your teeth?"

"Because they are opposite each other."

Paul would love this woman who so nearly followed his advice: *Give thanks in all circumstances, for this is God's will for you . . .* [I Thess. 5:13]

We all know the other kind who will find fault in all things, no matter what, like the son whose father recounted what he had done for him: "Six years ago I bought you a car, four years ago I paid off your college loan, two years ago I paid for your wedding and last year I paid the down payment on your house," to which the son replied, "Yes, but what have you done for me lately?"

It's easy to be a "two kinds of people guy." You just sort people into piles. Make one pile for thankful people, one pile for ungrateful people, one pile for pessimists and another pile for optimists, Etc. But a problem arises when you have to sort out an optimistic ingrate and a pessimistic thankful person. Which pile do you put which in? And what difference does it make, anyway? I thought you'd never ask!

For one thing it can make a difference in our health. The medical world was shaken up around forty years ago when researchers proved that our emotions can directly affect our physical bodies. A simple illustration is the tear drop. The chemical composition of a tear of sorrow is different from the chemistry of a tear of joy—emotion changing physiology. Attitudes can affect the cells of our immune system and thus our overall health.

But more than our immune system is at stake. Our social system is, too. The people around us seem to change with our moods. I was in my doctor's waiting room years ago and there was just one other person waiting there. We looked at each other and she said, "I think the whole world is sick these days."

And then there was this farmer sitting on a stone wall when a man stopped his car and said, "I'm moving from Oldplaceville back there and want to settle in Newplaceville up ahead. Can you tell me what kind of people to expect?"

"What kind of people were back there?"

"Oh they were selfish, pessimistic, and griping. That's why I'm leaving."

"Well," said the man on the wall, "You'd better keep right on going, because the people in the town ahead are just like the people you left behind."

Later another man stopped his car and asked a similar question. The farmer went through the same routine, ending with, "What kind of people were in the town you left?"

"Oh," said the pilgrim, they were honest, pleasant and hard working. I hated to leave."

The farmer said, "You'll be glad to know that the people in the next town are the same as those you are forced to leave."

Having established that there are two kinds of people [at least] the question arises: can they help being what they are? Are they born that way, or do they get that way? Social scientists have been arguing this point for centuries. I have to take the "get that way"side, else what use is it to preach a sermon. If they were born that way—destined to be that way—preaching at them would be an exercise in futility. And wouldn't it be mean of God to make people who cannot be good no matter how they try, and then call us preachers to exhort them to be good.

So, staying in form, I say there are two kinds of preachers, hopeful and pessimistic. The latter would be something like Winnie the Pooh's donkey friend, Eeyore, saying in his lugubrious tone of voice, "Ohhh, welll, I never thought my preaching would do any good anyway."

I'm of the former type. I've been called an incurable optimist, as though it were some sort of disease. I call it faith. I look out at the congregation. They are present in body. That's a fact. Their eyes are open as they look at me. That's a fact. I believe they are listening to me. That's faith.

There are two kinds of people, those who read the newsletters I send and those who do not.

I know which kind you are.

Thanks.

In Praise of Forgetting

Let's hear it for forgetting! For too long the art of forgetting has taken a back seat to remembering. The laurels have mostly gone to intellectual athletes who demonstrate prodigious feats of memory. For instance: who with a poor memory gets on Alex Trebek's show, Jeopardy? Who with unused memory skills graduates from high school and gets into college? Who with little ability to recall script lines becomes noted in the field of Broadway drama?

And even the Bible makes more of remembering than forgetting by a ratio of fifty to one: *Remember the Sabbath, remember the promises made to our Father Abraham, remember Lot's wife, remember the poor, etc.* Only the Apostle Paul recognizes the worth of forgetting with his words *Forgetting what is behind and straining forward to what lies ahead, I press on toward the goal to win the prize for which God has called me* [Philippians 3:13,14]

And to put the cherry on the Sunday, the government gets into the act and creates a holiday dedicated to memory—Memorial Day. It's unfair to we who have selective memories! You laugh, but sometimes it is better to forget than to remember. Consider the golf widow, she says to her husband, "You think more of golf than you do of me. I'll bet you don't even remember the day of our wedding!"

"Of course I do! How silly," he said. "That was the day I sank that forty-two-foot putt."

How much better off he'd have been had he forgotten all about that putt!

So, since very little attention has been paid to the benefits of forgetting, and since I am recognized for my abilities in that regard [see next paragraph], I thought I'd write something about it.

I once forgot a funeral I was to officiate at. It was a service for Hazel, the church secretary, an old and beloved friend. When I got home from teaching at the college, Polly asked me, "How did the funeral go?" I can't fully describe my consternation, my abject misery of the moment, or with what trepidation I knocked at the door of her relatives, not having the least idea of what to say, or if there even was anything to say. You won't believe what happened. The door opened and the person said, "Oh, Reverend! We're so glad to see you! We heard a siren during the funeral and we all were worried that you'd been in an accident and were being taken to the hospital! We're having some spaghetti. Won't you join us?" And I did. And we had a wonderful time.

Forgetting is not always a negative thing—as when it involves overlooking hurts, slights, insults and the like. Forgiving is a form of forgetting in which God helps us shake the moths out of our resentment closet.

There was once a priest who had told a whopping lie, and though he prayed for forgiveness, he carried a load of guilt around. Then a certain nun was assigned to the parish convent who had a reputation for walking and talking with Jesus. Now the priest worried lest, in talking with Jesus, she would discover the thing he had done. He engaged her in conversation. "Sister, when you talk with Jesus, do you ever mention me?"

"Oh, yes," she said," I mention all of you.

"The next time you pray," said the priest, "will you ask Jesus if there is anything I need to do to be right with him?"

The priest didn't sleep and hardly ate waiting to see if he would be found out. The next time they met, he asked the nun, "Sister, did you ask Jesus about me?"

"Yes," she said.

"What did he say," asked the priest, digging his fingernails into the palms of his hands.

"He said there was something, but he forgot what it was."

I am he that blotteth out thy transgressions and will not remember thy sins. [Isaiah 43:25] We need to forget our hurts and peeves involving others like God does with us. Do not we pray often *Forgive me my sins as I forgive those who sin against me?* If we forgive the sins of others against us, God will forgive us our sins against him. Quite a bargain.

Now let us consider what it would be like if God had created us so that we never forgot anything. If we couldn't forget there would be no need for such a word as memory, for memory means not forgetting. We then wouldn't be able to appreciate what a beautiful thing memory is because there. would not be such a concept. I'm sure God knew that we would be far worse off without a forgettery.

As a matter of fact there is a brain condition in which a person loses the ability to forget anything. It is an excruciating condition in which one's head seems to be one big bee hive of buzzing data with the victim unable to separate what happened a minute ago from what happened yesterday or ten years ago. It is all one big salad being stirred constantly. Only strong medication can enable the person to function.

So, we don't want to remember everything and neither do we want to forget everything. Forgetting may be as important as remembering—so we should appreciate the gift of forgetting bit more.

Let's hear it for a new national holiday.

Forgetting Day!

I Would Rather Be Right . . .

. . . than president," orated Henry Clay, the Great Compromiser, which possibly could be sour grapes, since he twice ran for the presidency (1832 & 1844) and lost. But he occupies a pedestal in the hearts of Americans, anyway. He was for many years the Speaker of the House and in that position was at least partially responsible for bringing our country to it's greatness.

Since Clay's times there have probably been White House occupants who would rather be president than right, but that remains for another discussion.

In general, who does not want to be right? I can think of one man. He rushed up to the trainman and gasped, "Quick, which way for the train to Brighton?" The coy trainman said, "If you go right you'll be left." The man thought a moment then dashed to the left and caught his train.

That incident excepted, all of us want to "go right." To be thought wrong by others can be a bummer.

In particular is this true for children. Some parents are quick to pick up on the "wrongs" of their children and slow to notice and comment on their "rights." This builds in them a shaky image of their worth to the world.

What are some of the ways we want to be right? (I thought you'd never ask!) One of the ways we want to be right is in our judgments. Henry Clay judged rightly that slaves should be free. Not all agreed with him, but he held his ground. Another way we want to be right is in our actions. Here Henry waffled. He owned slaves—and he freed them—but only after he died, when he would not have to face the results of his actions. He freed them through a stipulation in his will. Right judgments is the basis for wisdom; right judgments supported by right actions is the basis for greatness.

Righteousness is right action. Right and righteous come from the same Latin root *rectus* from which comes rectitude. For some reason I can't fathom—or maybe am afraid to fathom—I never wanted to be righteous. Righteous sounds too much like saintly, and that's the last thing I want to be called. Yet I probably will be called that in the end, because as soon as you put people in caskets, they are transformed into saints.

Which reminds me (nothing to do with this article), never make friends with an undertaker—he'll always let you down in the end.

The next time you open your mouth to prove someone wrong, stuff your fist in it and remember, "We are born with our eyes closed and our mouths open, and we spend the rest of our lives trying to reverse that mistake of nature."

Another right—one filled with controversy—is right religious beliefs—called orthodoxy, *ortho* for straight plus *doxy* for belief. Who has the authority to say which beliefs are right and which wrong? Usually it is a group of church officials called the hierarchy, *hier* for sacred plus *archy* for authority. One who holds a belief contrary to the judgment of the hierarchy is called a heretic, and must bring that belief into line or risk expulsion from the religious group.

The outstanding example of this in action is seen in the Roman and Spanish inquisitions in the middle ages. Thousands of Christians were burned at the stake for refusing to bend their beliefs—beliefs which seemed right to them—to the will of the inquistadors. Even if a person recanted, he could spend years in jail or lose all his property. It is sobering to me to realize that the popes and cardinals, during all the years of the inquisitions, felt beyond a shadow of a doubt that they were right, and the one on trial wrong, yet from our vantage point in history, we know the inquisitions themselves to be wrong. Can we be sure at any time that we are right?

I think not, at least as far as beliefs go. I have had a not inconsequential number of readers of these letters write to ask that their names be taken from the mailing list due to some positions I have espoused that differed from theirs. They might not expect to see me in heaven, but you have heard, I'm sure, the little story of the three surprises. I got to heaven and looked around. I was surprised that so-and-so was not there. I thought sure she'd make it. Then I saw so-and-so and was even more surprised. I never thought he'd get in. And then the biggest surprise of all. I made it!

It's easier to be sure of right actions than of right beliefs. We have the ten commandments, the constitution, the supreme court, etc. to keep us straight. Davy Crockett's motto in the War of 1812 said:

I leave this rule for others when I'm dead,
Be always sure you're right—then go ahead.

So I guess I'll go ahead. If I committed a wrong or two here, well, two wrongs make a right, don't they? That's what Mr. And Mrs. Wong told me. They named a child "Write," just to prove that two Wongs can make a Write.

Think it's the *right* time to go.

Building Bridges

Edwin Booth, the tragedian actor had a broken nose. A fan once remarked to him, "I love your acting, Mr. Booth, but I can't get over your nose." The great actor replied, "Of course not, madam, the bridge is broken."

Bridges mostly connect things, but I can't think of what the bridge of the nose connects except the lower nose and the forehead, but maybe it is like one child said, "God must have known we would need glasses cause look where lie put our ears and that bumpy place he put on our nose."

Another puzzle is why they named a card game "bridge." What does that connect? Someone said the purpose of bridge is to give people something to think about while they talk. I didn't say it! Someone else did. I'm only relating.

When bridges are broken or (burned behind us) people become cut off, alienated. When bridges are whole they connect things, facilitate things, make life more positive. Did you ever hear of a mean guy building a bridge to get back at somebody? But I want to talk about the kind of bridge that spans a river. And I want to use it as a metaphor for that bond which can exist between people—can link them together like the letter you are reading links you to Sacred Agent 007, a bridge that creates togetherness in a world that seems to foster alienation.

One of my favorite poems illustrating the need for bridges to span the generation gap is called *The Bridge Builder*.

An old man going a lone highway,
Came in the evening, cold and gray,
To a chasm vast and deep and wide
Through which was flowing a sullen tide.

The old man crossed in the twilight dim;
The sullen stream. had no fears for him;
But he turned when safe on the other side
And built a bridge to span the tide.

"Old man," said a fellow-traveler near,
"You're wasting your strength by building here;
You've already crossed the raging tide;
Why build you this bridge at eventide?"

The pilgrim lifted his old grey head.
"Good friend, on the path I have come," he said,
"There followed after me today
A youth, whose feet must pass this way.

This chasm that has been naught to me
To that fair-haired youth may a pitfall be.
I've already crossed in the twilight dim;
Good friend, I'm building this bridge for him."

When we lead lives of courage and integrity in the midst of adversity and temptation, we build bridges. We call such bridges positive role models. They make it easier for those who come after us to drearn and to dare. Role models, even the finest of them, are not saints. Saints don't make mistakes [I suspect]. Ordinary humans do, for to err is human. It's what these humans do about their mistakes and temptations that make them either role models or stumbling blocks. The lack of role models, i.e. bridge builders, is blamed for the frayed condition of our country's moral fibre. Ask anyone and they will point out several persons who are something less than bridge builders and role models. But beware of pointing fingers. When you point a finger at someone, three fingers are pointing back at you. I just decided not to point. Instead maybe I'll look in the mirror.

Maybe I need to take an "open *Book* quiz." Am I the Levite or the Samaritan when I come to the half-dead man on the Jericho toad? Do I take costly ointment and use it to anoint Jesus' feet or do I sell it and put the money in stocks and bonds for the future? Do I feed the hungry, clothe the naked, visit the sick? *For if you have done it unto the least of of these* . . . Said the greatest bridge builder of all time.

One of his disciples is alive and well and living in Montreal. He is Jean-Marc Trudel, one of God's great role models. John spends more time than most people have, it seems, to work in prisons, in crippled children's homes, in the church and with the suicide hot line. He comes down to the Singing Church two or three times each year. "I look forward to it," he says, "I feel so close to God there." He wrote a poem about the Great Bridge Builder:

> *I have these hands to lift you and help you, But they nailed them to the tree; I have these feet to come to you, But they, too, were nailed to the tree; I have this heart to love you, But they stilled it with a spear. I have no hands or feet or heart To do my work But yours.*

A mother was teaching her little girl to be a bridge builder. "It's not nice to hit your little brother. Go over and make peace. Say you're sorry." The little girl did and the mother said, "Now what have you learned about hitting?"

"I've learned that every time I hit somebody I'm supposed to say I'm sorry."

Don't Worry About It

The Chief of Service of Presbyterian Hospital in New York was making rounds with his interns. They came to the bed of a woman who was a victim of cancer. The intern in charge of her case went to her side, looked at her chart, held her hand and then in response to her question said, "About six months. But don't worry about it." And the group went on. Out of earshot of the patients the chief drew the student doctors close about him and addressed that intern. "You have just failed," he said. "Not for today but for the whole course. This is the end of your medical career. I want you to leave us now, go to your locker, pick up your clothes and check out." Never was there a more dejected figure than that intern as he walked away. Before he got out of earshot the doctor called out, "But don't worry about it." He called the young man back and said, "You have to understand more than medicine; you have to understand your patients. They continued rounds and I dare say that intern learned a lesson he would never forget.

To understand means to stand under, to support persons where they are weakest. Have you been tempted to say to someone who was going through trying times, "Don't worry about it?" I have and I guess you have, too. You were not "standing under" that person in his trying times. Having said that I must tergiversate (please, not on my new rug!) and talk of cliches of which the title of this letter is one.

Cliches show a lack of thought, they show a lack of concern and they can even be dangerous. I admit, however, that a large portion of our daily communication would dwindle to a trickle were we to eliminate cliches. They are the yeast in the dough of our communication, they expand it and puff it up. Speaking without thinking too deeply is better than not speaking at all. It passes the time of day and seems to answer some need in all of us for togetherness. And we can hardly be together in silence for very long. It can become awkward—even in a crowded elevator. Imagine coming to church, speaking to no one, worshiping, leaving, shaking hands with the minister, but all the time not saying a word. Can't be! Impossible! We're not built that way. But wait, the Quakers do it, don't they? They speak only to God during the service and wait till they are outside before speaking to each other. One Quaker couple spoke as they left the meeting house. The wife said, "Sometimes I think the whole world is daft except thee and me—and sometimes I wonder about thee!" But I wander.

Cliches can show a lack of love or concern for other people. This is what got the intern on the hot seat. He showed very little TLC. He understood his patient clinically—he knew about cancer, but he did not know her feelings, her hopes and fears. He got out of one jam with a cliche but the cliche got him right into another jam, dealing with patients without thinking.

When I assign a topic to students asking them to give it their most creative thought, and a paper is turned in that is obviously copied from beginning to end, I feel cheated. I feel that the student thought so little of me that second-hand stuff was good enough. Such a paper, itself, is a "cliche." Cliche-ing right back I write *So what else is new*? and I mark it with an F.

And cliches can actually be dangerous. Pearl Harbor is a prime example of this. At 7:50 AM on the morning of December 7, 1941, 353 Japanese planes sank several US ships, damaged 6 airfields and killed two thousand four hundred young American men. Fifty minutes earlier, 7:00 AM, while the attacking planes were still 137 miles away, two US soldiers sat in a small radar station out on the pacific. They saw some spots—blips—on the radar screen. Then there were more and soon the screen was filled with them. They went to the Duty Officer and reported. He was the newest and youngest officer in the unit, the low man on the totem pole. He had drawn this Sunday duty so the others could have shore leave. Without thinking he assumed the blips on the screen must be American planes and said to the radar operators, "Don't worry about it!"

So, children, as Howdy Doody would say, "Which cliche are we not going to use any more?" That's right! DON'T WORRY ABOUT IT!

I see I am running a little long on this letter. I'll have to go back and cut out a few words and sentences. You won't know which ones though, so don't worry about it.

Glimpses of Glory

I was reading one of Bob Thaves Frank and Ernest cartoons in which a doctor is in his examination room with Ernest. Ernest is telling the doctor that he has had an out-of-body experience. The doctor, looking at Ernest's humongous, flabby body, says, "I don't blame you."

That wasn't very nice of the doctor to make fun of his patient that way, but it was amusing. The doctor represents those who poke fun at people who claim to have actually had a glimpse of Heaven as they neared life's exit door. Unlike that doctor, however, if someone tells me they have had an out-of-the-body experience, I am inclined to believe them; maybe because of my experience in this area.

During over twenty years of teaching Death and Dying courses at Northern Essex Community College, I got to know personally more than a thousand students. Many of them, after the class was under way, and they began to feel safe from people like the doctor, they would tell of their own experience and say, "I never talk about this because I am afraid people will laugh." It was obvious in their telling that the experience went way beyond any earthly happening. I became convinced of the reality of such events and still am. Let me relate one of these.

A student said one night, "I'd like to tell you about something that happened to me. I was at a Celtics game when I had a heart attack. I managed to get myself out of the building and to the Massachusetts General Hospital. The last words I heard the medical people say were *We're not going to save this one.* The next thing was, like everybody says, the brilliant white light and a sensation that would be like all the ecstasies I ever felt put together. I was in rapture, leaping and shouting—without a body somehow. Then out of the light came a profound sense of *presence.* There was nothing I could see, only an awareness. Something or someone spoke to me—not words—just an impression like ESP. I can't communicate to you the words but I know what they meant. It was like "How did you love?" Then I remembered what a bastard I had been. I had alienated my wife and children and even my father. I had climbed over anyone who got in the way of my success. Now the unspoken words were telling me I had to go back. I was sick. I fought.

I begged. But I was being pushed somehow and then there were those faces around the hospital table. They were filled with a wonder like *look what we did*, but only I knew who had done it, really.

"I felt love, different than I ever felt before, a warm love, right there, love for each of the medical people. When I recovered, I went to my wife and told her of my experience and asked for her forgiveness. I went to one of my sons. He was under his car fixing its starter. He crawled out and stood. I embraced him and said *Son, I love you.* He dropped his wrench and just stared. I went to my father in the nursing home and said, *Dad, I love you.* 'No you don't,' he said and turned toward the wall. Twice more I visited him with the same results. The third time I took his hand and said *Let's pray.* For a long moment he was silent and then he said, 'Well, maybe you do,' and we had a prayer together.

"Since that time I have been telling everyone how important love is, and to get ready, for the most wonderful experience that awaits them. Once since then I had another heart attack, and when I woke up, I was disappointed. I really wanted to go."

I'm thankful for the students who shared such events with the class. I believed in heaven before I taught those classes and believe even more now. But unlike Jim, I'm not eager to go today. Maybe I'm like the girl in Sunday School. The teacher was talking about heaven. She paused and asked, "How many would like to go to heaven?" All but this one girl held up their hand.

"Don't you want to go to heaven, dear?"

"I do, but Mommy said I have to come right home after Sunday School."

Elisabeth Kubler-Ross writes that one of the glories of this experience is the loved ones waiting to welcome us, and, she says, "*Only people who have died are there to greet us when we go*!" She tells of a girl who made this glory trip and saw her father there welcoming her with open arms, but something drew her back to life. She said, "Daddy was there and I wanted to stay with him, it was all so wonderful. But I know he couldn't be there, 'cause he's not dead yet." A few hours later it was learned that her father, rushing to get to his daughter's bedside, was in a fatal car crash. Wow! Is heaven's glory real, or what!

Charles Gabriel wrote a hymn about that: *Oh That Will Be Glory for Me!* It was the most popular hymn of its time. When he would lead a revival, singing this hymn, his face would beam and they called him Old Glory Face. Remember the words? *When all my labors and trials are o'er, and I am safe on that beautiful shore, just to be near the dear Lord I adore, will through the ages be glory for me.*

Boy! Do I want to go there but not just yet—not till I get this letter in the mail.

Gods Busy Work

In one of Bob Thaves' Frank and Ernest cartoons, God is shown in heaven going over his plans and specifications for the earth he is about to create. One of his assistant angels says, "Making all the fingerprints different I can understand, but doing it for snowflakes! Isn't that just busy work?"

I Guess I have to go along with the angel. Why does God go to such great lengths to make everything he creates different? Each grain of sand, each rock, each hair on our head, each sparrow, each tree? There has to be a reason. I wish I knew what it was, but I never will. Yet I can't help speculating and conjecturing.

Speculate arises from the Latin *speculari* to watch from a distance, and conjecture is from the Latin *conjicere* to pile things together to see what can be made out of them. So from a distance we make observations, gather data, then pile them together and begin to imagine, to conjecture—a wild and wonderful game God built into every human.

The conjecture game started with Creation. Eve had the first move. She plucked a round, red, object from a tree, showed it to Adam and said, "I wonder what this is?" And Adam, having the next move, said, "I'll bite," and the game continues to this day.

A parent says to a child, "Don't stick anything into that electric outlet!" And what does the child do? He conjectures: "I wonder what would happen?"and when the parent's back is turned will try to find out. So, when God said *You are free to eat from any tree in the garden, but you must not eat from the tree of the knowledge of good and evil*, I believe he knew what a short life-span the apple would enjoy.

Watch any very young animal and you will know immediately that God must be a fun-loving parent. He made curiosity, exploration, adventure, a part of every animal—the basis of play. To we humans he added something: conjecture—the ability to *play mentally*—to take things apart and put them together in new ways—exploring with our minds. Perhaps other animals do this. What's going on in the mind of a dog, for instance, when it cocks its head to one side and looks at us? Maybe I don't want to know.

Conjecture is a priceless commodity. It's made more precious by the possibility of its absence. Things can go wrong genetically and hormonally in the reproductive process, things which result in a brain that cannot wonder. What a tragedy! I saw this in Ralph, a 22-year-old shriveled up patient of mine on C ward of the Concord State Hospital many years ago. We would prop him up with pillows so he could look out the window at the wonders of God's nature. How much of this he appreciated we never knew, for his total vocabulary consisted of one word, "Duh."

At the end of one's living—having experienced the myriad miracles of life—Alzheimers can begin to eat away at the structure of memory, severing the cords of communication and intimacy. We're tempted to say, "What a lousy world!"

But God's busy work created the best world that could be created and still allow for freedom and choice, for without freedom of choice there could be neither curiosity nor conjecture for both are predicated on the freedom of the mind. If God were less busy and simply kept all choice for himself, we would be puppets and he the puppet master, determining every word we utter and every movement we make. "Playing" a game under those circumstances, would be making moves dictated by a power outside ourselves—moves would be mechanical—always the same outcome. With freedom God gives us curiosity, conjecture, exploration, invention, etc. What invaluable gifts!

So thanks for your busy work, God—especially when you are busy helping us move through life.

Gender Neutral

Art Sansom writes a comic strip called *The Born Loser*. In one strip he has a precocious child of about eight years of age approaching her pastor with question: "How about the male bias in our church?"

"Ah, yes," said the pastor, "we have taken care of that with more gender neutral language!"

"Then how come," said the youngster, "you keep referring to the songs as hims?"

A minister once asked, "Who would like to choose the first hymn?" and an unmarried woman jumped up and said, "I'll take him and him and him."

We can all laugh at that, but there is a serious campaign under way to make our orders of worship, statements of faith and hymnals gender neutral—politically correct. We're in something of a turmoil about this because people get set in their ways. Every time a major new version of the Bible is introduced we hear, "Let's go back to the good old days. The King James was good enough for Paul and Silas and it's good enough for me." Remember when the Catholic Church began saying the mass in English? The "old-timers" wanted none of it. "Let's go back to the Latin," they said, "the language of God." I'm one of those old-timers. I'm a little set in my ways. It is going to bother me to say, "Our Parent who art in heaven," or to sing, "O Creator, *when I in awesome wonder consider all the worlds thy hands have made*." But I'm going to try to change because I acknowledge the injustice that has been done to women for thousands of years. Unwittingly we have relegated them to powerlessness. Look at the titles of power: Lord and Lady, God and Goddess, King and Queen, Emperor and Empress. The top-dog, bottom-dog reality is obvious.

What's wrong with God being thought of as "father," as male? Well, for one thing, fathers have been dominating, possessive, powerful for thousands of years while weak. mothers were submissive, giving and weak. Every male Jew says a ritual morning prayer "0 Lord, I thank thee that thou didst not make me a woman." It strikes me as humorous to think of Joseph saying that prayer each morning as he and Mary were on their way to Bethlehem. And in the ancient Greek and Roman civilizations the father was called

Patria Potestes, the powerful father. He owned his wife and children. He could sell them, imprison them, kill them.

So what's wrong is, calling God "father"gives him gender; lowers him to the rank of human. And the word "father"conjures up some pretty awful images in the minds of abused children; hardly the figure a boy or girl would want to pray to. And of course if there is a father, where is the mother? In Semple's book *Children's Letters to God*, one child wrote: "I read your name in the Bible a lot, but I don't read about Mrs. God. Is there some way you could let us know?" (Signed: Maria) That would be a big help, Maria. If we knew there was a Mrs. God, we wouldn't have to change our ritual as much. The Catholic Church got around this neatly by deifying Mary, the mother of our Lord. If the Catholic theologians revamp their prayer book, it would be easy for them to say, "Our parents who art in heaven."

I think the creator will be pleased when we stop calling him God. He gave his name to Moses at the burning bush: I AM THAT I AM. And later when Moses talked with I Am on Mount Sinai, the divine name was revealed to him: YHWH. When we read the name God in the Old Testament, this is it. The customary vowels used to make the name pronounceable were A and E, YAHWEH. When Moses come down from the mountain his face shone as though he had been involved in a nuclear accident. The people knew he had seen God. They were in awe. They were so impressed that they never pronounced that name. Only the priest could do that and then only after a cleansing ritual. Maybe we should be informed by this. Why should we, YAHWEH'S people, be satisfied with a generic term that is used to describe all the gods of all the cultures and of a l l the ages?

Instead of gender-neutral words in worship and song why not substitute a humming sound, a Hmmm for each syllable that might offend. We could then sing: "Oh hmmm my hmmm, when I in awesome wonder. and "Praise Hmmm from whom all blessings flow, praise Hmmm all creatures here below; praise hmmm above, ye heavenly host; praise Hmm, hmm, and Holy Ghost." But I suppose Imogene would even think Hmmm sounds too masculine. Oh, well, you come up with a better one.

Have a Heart

Did you ever wonder why the four suits in a deck of cards are called clubs, diamonds, hearts and spades? Neither did I till just now when I began to compose this article on February, valentines, hearts and love. It seems to me that they might stand for four aspects of human endeavor: clubs (conflict and fighting), diamonds (possessions and wealth), hearts (emotion and love) and spades (building and work). And how about their ranking? Does it reflect some kind of unconscious value judgment? Clubs (conflict) ranks lowest; then diamonds (wealth), then hearts (love) and highest of all; spades (work).

Enough speculation. I want to talk about hearts. It is hard to imagine a conversation, essay or sermon that doesn't use the word. Hard-hearted, soft-hearted, cold-hearted, warm-hearted, true-hearted, heart of gold, heart of steel, heartache, heartbroken, a person after my own heart, heart in the right place, my heart is yours, I lost my heart to him or her, my heart was in my mouth, heart and soul, and I could go on to fill the rest of this page. Why is the word heart so pervasive in our language?

In the study of linguistics a sociologist can rank the values of a society by the number of ways they use the words of their language. Eskimos, for instance, have fourteen definitions for snow. We have only one (though when we suffer a nor'easter with twenty inches of snow I hear a few more words I can't put in this letter. The first thing a little Eskimo child learns is: "Don't eat yellow snow." Snow is obviously of supreme importance to them.

But while Eskimos have one definition for heart we have twenty-seven. Our language is saturated with words that have to do with love and the heart. "How do I love thee? Let me count the ways," wrote Elizabeth Barrett Browning to her husband, Robert, thereby picturing for all of us one of the great love relationships of all time.

> I love thee to the depth and breadth and height
> My soul can reach, when feeling out of sight
> For the ends of Being and ideal Grace.
> I love thee to the level of every day's
> Most quiet need, by sun and candle-light.
> I love thee freely, as men strive for right.

I love thee purely, as they turn from praise.
I love thee with the passion put to use
In my old griefs, and with my childhood's faith.
I love thee with a love I seemed to lose
With my lost saints—I love thee with the breath,
Smiles, tears, of all my life! And, if God choose,
I shall but love thee better after death.

Most of us cannot be so eloquent. When Robert Browning stormed into the life of Elizabeth Barrett she was a thirty-nine-year-old invalid. At an early age she injured her spine and her father made a recluse of her (for her own good, of course). He vowed never to let Elizabeth marry. A part of the love story is how Robert whisked her away, married her secretly and then took her to Italy where they lived till she died. He then wrote *Prospice,* one of the greatest poems about love and death ever written.

Words of love can be beautiful, meaningful and therapeutic. But they can also be empty and calculating, as when a young man says to his date, "I love you," when he really means, "I love me and I want you." Or when a heart swelling with emotion spews out the love word like an automatic weapon. One young man sent his sweetheart a telegram: "I love you, I love you, I love you. John." The telegraph operator said, "You used only nine words; you are allowed ten." The young man picked up the pen and wrote: "I love you. I love you. I love you. Regards. John."

Love is emotion but it is more. It is also an intellectual endeavor. Socrates, the patron saint of philosophy, believed that love was the universal undergirding force. The very name philosophy is made from two words *philos* and *sophia* love and knowledge. He reasoned that love was the universal process, the dynamo, that drives us and pulls us to the ultimate reality of truth, goodness and beauty. Philosophy to Socrates was an internal dialogue between feelings and duty—between what we desire to do and what we ought to do. He said, "The unexamined life is not worth living."

Like Socrates, Jesus said little about the emotion of loving but his life said a lot about the action of loving. Jesus knew that real loving is hard, often painful and could lead to death, as it did for him. *Greater love has no one than this, that he lay down his life for his friends*, he said. And he did. And Socrates did.

And Paul did. Before he died, a prisoner in Rome, his head was placed on the chopping block many times because of his love for Jesus and for all those who should know Jesus but didn't. Although he wrote some of the most beautiful words ever written about love, they were words calling love to action. He wrote:

Love is patient and kind,
And bears up under pain and disappointment.
Love is courteous, and trusting;
Love is not envious;

Love is unpretentious and generous;
Love is cool-headed and unselfish;
Love does not hold a grudge but is quick to forgive.
Love endures.

Spoken love can be as empty as the air currents that carry the words. Action love never is. That is why John, the Beloved Disciple, left us his interpretation of love: *Dear children, let us not love with words or tongue but with actions and in truth.*

Not that words of love are necessarily bad. A wife complained to the divorce court judge, "He never says he loves me," to which the husband replied, "I told her twenty-seven years ago that I loved her and I haven't changed my mind!"

One of my life-long idols, Toyohiko Kagawa, tried to walk the path of Jesus in the slums of Kobe. He gave his coat to a shivering wanderer, contracted pneumonia and lost the use of one lung. He took into his room a sick man, to nurse him, caught an eye disease and lost the use of one eye. But that good eye could still express love. One day a mother brought to him her baby who was near death. The Japanese Christian held the child and prayed. When it seemed that there was no more hope he hung his head. A tear from his good eye ran down and fell on the closed eyelid of the baby. It opened its eyes and began to grow strong again.

Have a heart Then go forth to work and love as Jesus worked and loved—without haste—and without rest.

How Do You Plead

Two deacons were having a drink at a bar when they saw the preacher go by. One became very upset and said, "I sure hope he didn't see us!" "Why?" said the other, "God knows we're here." "Yeah," said the first, "but God won't tell my wife." Guilt. Usually, when we feel guilty, it is because we have broken one of the ten commandments. Or, as in the above case we have broken a wife's commandment. We know where we have gone wrong. But what about guilt we feel when we know we have not broken a commandment, as in the following incident. I was kneeling in the sand, building castles. Patrick, my grandson was there to make it legitimate. A father and son came down the steps nearby and proceeded to another part of the beach. The boy was acting in a way that drew my attention. It was the tilt of the head, the unusual way he felt the wall, the unsteady walk and the clenched fist moving up and down, uncontrollably beating his chest. The father studiously avoided looking at us as they walked by and didn't say a word. But I think I could read his mind: "Why is that little boy so normal, so full of promise, so excited as he exercises his creative abilities, and my boy is a prisoner of a body he can't control and a mind with the light turned out?" A wave of guilt washed over me. I prayed silently, "Why, God? Why have I been given normal children and grandchildren while so many others have been given the superhuman task of caring for the "little birds with broken wings."

It wasn't the first time I had felt this. It comes over me when on the evening news I see starving people and I think of my bounteous table. I sense it when our country turns back the boat people or rounds up other "illegals"and ships them back to the country from which they fled. The same feeling floods in when I drive through an impoverished neighborhood. They cannot even afford a car. I think of my apartment with its picture window overlooking the Atlantic. Their rooms often have no window at all.

Why should I feel guilty about these things? There is no cause and effect connection between my behavior and their misery. It has been called existential guilt, the guilt that is implicit in the fact that I exist. Maybe there's a window through which we can glimpse an answer. Its in Cain's response to God who questions him. "Where is your brother,

Abel?" and Cain replies in effect, "How should I know? Am I my brothers keeper?"' We might not be our brother's keeper, but we are our brother's brother. We all have the same father. We are family. When others in the family are sick, lost, or hungry, we feel it, we care. The concern is built in at the factory.

Moses illustrates this in one place: *If in the land which the Lord your God gives you to possess, if any one is found slain, lying in the open country, and it is not known who killed him, then your elders and judges shall come forth and they shall measure the distance to the cities around him; and the elders of the city nearest the slain man shall take upon themselves the guilt of the slayer.*

Even though I am not directly responsible for the misery in the world, there's a tape measure between me and those experiencing it, and God whispers, "Do something.

I do something when in my imagination I take on the pain, when I weep because of it. But I do more when I put money in the offering plate, when I make my pledge out for more than I had originally planned, when I send a check to Americares, to Friends Service Committee or some other charity. And I do something when I pray. As Tennyson said, "For so the whole round earth is every way bound by gold chains about the feet of God . . . ."

Seven days without prayer makes one weak. O'Shaugnesy would have been better off had he abided by that dictum. The magistrate said to him, "O'Shaugnesy, This is the third time you have come before me because of your disorderly conduct; how do you plead?" and O'Shaugnesy said as he knelt, "On my knees, your honor, on my knees!"

There is a famous statue of Christ in a Scandinavian Cathedral. The sculptor crafted it in such a way that the viewer has to be on his knees to appreciate the full compassion on that face. Visitors walk around it and remark on its beauty, but very often when they kneel and look up, tears come to their eyes. So it is with us. Whether we are pleading another's cause or our own, the lines of communication are more open when we kneel.

As one poet put it:
We mutter and sputter;
We fume and we spurt;
We mumble and grumble;
Our feelings get hurt.
We can't understand things;
Our vision grows dim,
When all that we need
Is a moment with HIM.

Guilty or not guilty, the greatest exercise known for strengthening the soul is getting on one's knees before the Lord. So, however you plead, do it on your knees.

I Wish It In My Heart

My five-year-old grandson, Patrick, and I were playing a game of Memory in which you pick up one card and then another. You look at the two pictures revealed, put them back down, trying to remember where you put them. Later, after several other pairs have been looked at and replaced, you try to match those same cards. With his young brain he always beats me, so I asked him how he managed to match up so many pictures, and his simple reply was, "I wish it in my heart."

What a definition of prayer! No words needed. Just pictures of what is desired. Healing for some person, peace in some country, shoring up a shaky marriage, food for a poor family, and on and on and on. The pictures could be elaborate or plain; they could be still or moving; they could be a single picture on a wall or a museum full of pictures. One thing they would be, I believe, is powerful. This is not a new idea, Adelaide Bry in *Directing the Movies of Your Mind*, has been using imaging techniques in healing for many years. She doesn't call her techniques prayer, but if we lift our mental pictures to God it is prayer. Verbal prayers will never be replaced, but there is room for other modes of prayer. Imaging prayer, I believe, is powerful as are also action prayers.

Polly and I learned about action prayers at a conference where Frank Laubach was the leader. He took us outdoors, pointed in the direction of Switzerland where a summit meeting of world leaders was going on. He prayed for guidance, for peace and for love. After each sentence we would act the prayer by taking our words in our hands and throwing them in the direction of the world conference. Silly? Childish? Maybe, but Jesus did say, *Anyone who will not receive the kingdom of God like a little child will never enter it.* To put it another way, sophistication will never unlock the gates to heaven. Carl Jung recalled the moment his life became coordinated and his knowledge began to fit into an overall cohesive framework. It was after watching his little son playing with some toys, completely absorbed in the activity, that he got down on his hands and knees and began "making believe" in the child's game. Word prayers will never be replaced, of course, nor should they. But If brevity (as Shakespeare wrote) is the soul of wit, maybe we should add sermons and prayers to the list.

Depth. in sermons and prayers is to be desired but length is not an asset. "How long should a man's legs be?" someone asked Abe Lincoln and he replied, "Just long enough to reach the ground." How long should a prayer be? Just long enough to reach the Lord. A mother was listening to her son's bedtime prayer. The boy got going on and on, praying for animals, relatives, friends, trees, etc. His mother finally said, "Could you hurry it up. I've got things to do." The lad ended his prayer with, "I'll see you later, God. Mom's getting itchy." God must have infinite patience, but even he must get itchy now and then when one of his children goes on a prayer spree. I'll still talk with God and I know he'll talk with me, but now and then when I have an especially serious request, I'll image it. I'll make a mental picture of it and "wish it in my heart."

Puttering Around

In an episode of Bill Waterson's Calvin and Hobbes the following conversation takes place between Calvin and Susie, an age mate he can't stand.

Calvin: I couldn't stand being a girl.
Susie: I can't stand you either way.
Calvin: When guys grow up, they get to play with cars, sports equipment, cameras, stereos, electric tools—you name it. But girls don't get any toys when they grow up. Women just buy clothes and shoes. How boring! How sad!
Susie: I guess girls actually mature as they get older.
Calvin: I can't wait till I'm old enough to putter around.

I think Calvin would have to admit that I'm old enough to begin "puttering around." Actually I think I've been puttering around most of my life. Here is my personal definition of puttering—one you won't find in any dictionary.

To putter means to spend one's time doing the things one "enjoys." I have been fortunate in that I have enjoyed doing *most of the things* I have done in my years on this planet. Notice the words in italics. There have been some tasks that don't fit my personal definition above—tasks that are repetitive, forced, boring jobs. Like peeling bushels of potatoes while on K.P. or walking guard duty, four hours on—four hours off. Instead of puttering, those things were muttering. I guess behavior ceases to be puttering when we have to clench our teeth and mutter.

A word about "enjoys." There is probably a better word to describe what I mean than that. I don't mean simply having fun. Like the mother at the carnival with her little child. The child was standing by her side glumly. The mother scolded her: "You wanted to come to the carnival and have fun; now you start having fun or I'll spank you till you do have fun!"

Maybe "finding fulfillment" better defines my kind of puttering. The pastor's life is definitely not all enjoyment. I certainly don't enjoy conducting funeral services. In fact they sometimes "destroy" me. One I remember so well. A ten-month-old boy, so beautiful, holding his teddy bear. The mother threw herself across the casket at the cemetery crying, "He'll be so cold, he'll be so cold!" The grandmother fainted and had to be taken away in an ambulance. And there was the one for the young man who was president of our youth group. He drowned while at the Sunday School picnic. His parents were not there and I had to go and break the news. That was a tough one!

But then on the flip side of the pastor's life are the weddings. One stands out. The groom was sixty-five. He was a widower. The bride was fifty, an "unclaimed blessing." Barely had I started: "Do you take . . . when she grabbed his arm, squeezed it, looked ecstatically into his face and said, "I do, I do, I do!"

Of course the things that I deem puttering, enjoyable, fulfilling and worthwhile are judged to be so because I am looking happily back at them. A survey on happiness was done about twenty years ago by a team of sociologists. The subjects were asked: "What part of your life would you say was the happiest of all?" You might be surprised at the answer: "When my children were small." I dare say that if you had asked those people the same question back when they actually were surrounded by tiny tots, you would have received a different answer. Hindsight always has 20-20 vision.

As I look over my shoulder everything seems like yesterday. And every single event, happy or sad, easy or difficult, seems like a piece of colored glass which when put in its proper place by the Infinite Artist, becomes a part of a beautiful stained glass window.

I've been puttering at writing this piece now for several hours, really enjoying it. Maybe it's high time I stopped puttering and did something more serious like sitting in my easy chair, snacking and working a crossword.

Sermons In Stomes

Shakespeare was not thinking of gravestones when he wrote: *Tongues in trees, books in running brooks, sermons in stones and good in everything*. But many a sermon has been preached on a memorial marker.

Where did the idea of gravestones come from? What is their purpose? The oldest "tombstones," the pyramids, were constructed by their eventual occupants. The purpose: to provide a secure and comfortable passage to the afterworld, safe from marauders and from the prying eyes of the living. The pyramid built by Cheops, at Gezeh, nearly 5,000 years ago, covered thirteen acres and was one of the Seven Wonders of the World.

Only the rulers and the wealthy could afford such a place of transition, such a rite of passage. Others were relegated to anonymity, the ultimate of which was the common grave, a large hole in the ground. As late as the 14th century in Europe, the "common" man was waked at the church then deposited in such a grave. Each body was covered with lime, and when the hole began to fill up with bodies, it would be filled in with dirt and another common grave dug.

Cemeteries range from small family ones, found where people live far apart, to Forest Lawn in California. They tend to reflect the nature of the social and class groupings that create them, such as the one in Bradford, Massachusetts created by the First Church of Christ in the middle 1600's. In the oldest part of that cemetery the foot of each grave points east. This is so that when Christ comes again (from the east as the Bible says) the deceased will arise facing him. Many things can be learned about the customs and beliefs of an era by viewing the writing, the engraving and the length of life recorded on the stones.

There is a modern trend of purchasing a lot and stone, including names engraved on the stone, before one dies. One couple, good friends of ours, did this and nearly precipitated my early demise. I was conducting a grave side service when I happened to glance at the next grave. There were their names on the stone. The people probably wondered if I swallowed a gnat or something as I gulped. That was many years ago and the couple are still very much with us, which cancels out any superstition about doing such things early on.

In California one can purchase a talking gravestone. It has a built-in tape player which, when a button is pressed, will give forth a ten-minute message from the deceased. I thought of doing that with my favorite sermon but then thought better of it. I couldn't find one that was only ten minutes long. And besides, I might want to change it after my departure.

If you can afford it, you can direct that you be cremated, your ashes encased in a stainless steel cylinder which will be released from a NASA flight. The living relatives can then look at the night sky, see a glint of light, and say, "There goes aunt Martha."

And of course there is cryogenics. You have your body frozen solid and packed into a temperature-controlled steel and glass container. It costs about forty thousand dollars. The idea is to be kept in this state until a cure is discovered for what caused your death. Then (it has not yet been tested) you will be carefully thawed and treated with the new medicine. But what if the end of the world comes before the new cure is found? One might get a rather cool reception in heaven me thinks.

I prefer the old fashioned cemetery. I even like to wander around reading the inscriptions on the stones. Some are humorous, some are serious and some are great poetry. There was a lawyer in England named John Strange. He was known for his honesty. When he died someone put this epitaph on his stone: "Here lies an honest lawyer, and that is Strange."

Another one I love was for a man who always treated his friends to dinner, and would never let the other person pick up the tab. A survivor who appreciated this placed a huge boulder on his grave—not at the head but right in the middle—and a brass plaque on the boulder read: "This one is on me."

One all-time favorite was written on the memorial stone of a hypochondriac: "I told you I was sick."

I need the humorous ones, for once in a while my heart is wrenched by one like that written by Mark Twain for one of his beautiful daughters.

Warm summer sun,
  Shine kindly here.
  Warm southern wind,
  Blow softly here.
Green sod above,
  Lie light, lie light.
Good night, dear heart,
  Good night, good night.

Gravestones are really constructed of heartaches, hopes and tears. Viewers of tombstones might wonder why some epitaphs are humorous and others somber. The answer, I believe, lies in the words of Abraham Lincoln whose philosophy reflects something of my own. He was asked by a friend why he persisted in telling humorous stories when all around was death and destruction. He replied: "If it weren't for laughter, my heart would break."

Someday you might walk through a cemetery and read:

> Sacred Agent 007
> Wrote his last church letter
> And has gone to Heaven.

He hopes.

Immunization

In 1796 Edward Jenner, a British physician, had a revelation. He treated people who had cowpox and he treated people who had smallpox. He noticed that milkmaids who had contracted cowpox by milking infected cows never came down with smallpox. He reasoned that there must be something in the pustules on the milkmaids' hands that immunized them against the related disease, smallpox. His now famous experiment of inoculating the 8-year-old James Phipps with material from the milkmaids' pustules changed the world. It immunized not only James Phipps, but millions of others after him against the dreaded and disfiguring disease, smallpox.

As I was reading about this in a science magazine recently, the thought entered my tickle box, wouldn't it be wonderful to have a vaccine against sin? We could inject a syringe full of minor sins into each child and they would then be able to live without sin. Seriously, though, there have been sincere efforts by religious leaders and institutions to develop programs to strengthen a person's will power (or won't power) in regard to withstanding temptation. I will mention three of these. I think they are fascinating and also instructive about human nature and our relationship with God. They are: the Jesuits' spiritual exercises, sanctification, and the Methodist class meeting.

In their training, young Jesuit priests spend hours memorizing Bible verses which, when uttered or thought (as temptation arises) help fight-off-the devil. Sort of like having a canister of Raid handy during mosquito season. The novitiates spend countless hours during their spiritual exercises trying to sin—in their imagination—and with each sin to respond immediately with the vaccine they memorized from the Bible. Thus they are prepared to *Put on the whole armor of God, that ye may be able to stand against the wiles of the Devil,* as the Apostle wrote to the Christians at Ephesus.

Sanctification, called a second work of Grace, is like a booster shot which makes one's salvation more impregnable. A note about the concept *saved. Save* is a verb, Salvation is a noun. They are related to the word salve (to heal or make whole). The word salver or tray is directly related to the word salve or save. It originates from the ancient practice of putting a piece of the roast the king was about to eat on a special tray (salver).

A designated eater would gobble this down (taking the place of the king, as it were) and if he kept on living, the king went ahead and ate the roast. The salver was used to salve or save the king. Being saved is the first work of grace. It starts the convert on a new path, but it doesn't mean the devil has been scared off forever. He might be back the very next day. This is where sanctification, the second work of grace, comes in. This inoculation is supposed to be comparable to driving the stake through the heart of the vampire.

To receive sanctification, one must make a second trip to the altar. I traveled that route more than once but never received the vaccine. I am therefore not holy (in case you wondered).

But some people did receive sanctification with great rejoicing. This led to one of the bitterest disappointments of my teen-age life. There was a man and a woman in our congregation who had received this grace. They were soloists in the choir and would melt our hearts when they sang a duet about the love of God. They were my idols. They claimed to have received sanctification and their spiritual lives seemed to prove it. Then they sinned and made public confession. I'll leave to your imagination the sin they committed. My ideal was shattered. My pastor, Esther Boyer, worked hard to keep me from losing my faith.

The Methodist Class Meeting was something like sanctification. Once a person was saved in one of John Wesley's revival meetings, they, too, found that they needed something more. This something more was the class meeting. Each new convert had to join a class, usually ten or twelve people. The classes met once a week or oftener and each member had to confess all sins and temptations he or she had experienced that week. Just knowing they had to do this was often enough to keep them from falling from grace. The class meeting was like the perfect family, a place of refuge and strength. I read some of the unpublished diaries of those class members. The love, the strength, the courage for living they provided were more valuable to them than they could fully describe. But even this was not enough to eradicate all sin from their lives.

So why didn't God build immunization into us at the factory? Why make life so difficult and often tragic when it could have been avoided? What would life have been like? No sin would mean no theft, no lies, no hate, no envy, no infidelity no soap operas. There would be no word "theft" in any language (or larceny, piracy, stealing, burglary either, for that matter). Such sins would be blocked out. There would be no temptation.

BUT on the other hand we could never be a pilgrim to progress through gross temptations and finally with all the fanfare of heaven enter those golden gates, show Saint Peter our scars and be congratulated as we are hugged by God, our maker.

With immunization we would have our sins ***blocked out***, but with salvation we would have them ***blotted out***. Somehow I think I prefer the latter.

In the Depths

Columbus first stepped on the American **mainland** in 1502 and named the spot Honduras, which means *depths,* after the deep waters off its coast. 496 years later, 1998, the people of Honduras were truly in the depths—not of the ocean but of despair—due to Hurricane Mitch, the deadliest storm to hit Honduras in 200 years, which left 6,500 people dead, 1,932,000 homeless and anther 427,000 living in shelters. That's what you call *in the depths.*

Section 729 in Roget's Thesaurus encompasses the category *Adversity.* Under his general classification is listed negative life events from *predicament* all the way up to *catastrophe.* If you are late for an appointment with your boss and can't find your car keys, that's a predicament, but if you are standing in a sea of mud, under which lies thousands of bodies, perhaps your own family, your whole village—that's a catastrophe. I've been watching these things on TV and felt I must write something about it, but how can I write about something so far beyond anything I have experienced? But then how can I *not* write about it?

I have to write about it because to not write about it is to hide from the questions which such human tragedies dangle in my face. They hang there, assailing me in thunderous silence. So I write, all the while knowing how impossible is my task. I will be like Icarus of mythology. Knowing humans were not built for flying, he tried it anyway. He constructed wings of wax and feathers and managed to fly till he got too close to the sun which melted the wax in his wings and sent him plummeting back to earth. So do me a favor, please; keep your eye on the sky in case the wax in my wings begins to melt. If you see me plummeting, run and get help.

Where is God when these catastrophes are happening? Where was God when the 1978 floods in India killed 15,000 people? When the 1998 earthquake in Armenia took 40,000 lives? When the 1991 cyclone in Bangladesh killed 139,000 persons? I believe he was there. I believe he was in Honduras when the mud buried a part of his creation. If he was there, why did he let it happen? I have a theory. Wait a sec while I put on my wings.

In the beginning God created the heaven and the earth [Gen. 1:1.] I think this says God created the universe **and the inexorable natural** laws (the laws of nature) which would govern that universe without any interference from him.

The Bible doesn't say so, but I think God was lonely. Something was missing. So *the Lord God formed man of the dust of the ground, and breathed into his nostrils the breath of life; and man became a living soul [Gen. 2:7]* Then God made two big mistakes—it seems to me. 1-) He gave us humans freedom of choice and 2-) put us in charge *and God said replenish the earth and subdue it and have dominion over it. Gen. 1:28)* He knew all the time, I'm sure, that this would be putting his children, his *piece de resistance,* on a collision course with nature. And I'm just as sure he knew the collisions, though devastating, would prove beneficial in the long haul. You and I can only dimly grasp how this could possibly be *for now we see through a glass darkly [I Cor. 13:12].*

What has this to do with Honduras? One scene out of that horror was of a lone man digging a hole in the mud. He dug deep—over his head. He dug long—morning till night. All this to retrieve a door, the door to a house he would never see again. He finally rescued the door. Money-wise the door was worth little, but this door would go on his new house someday. Following so humongous a loss, he didn't give up. The door gave him something to hold on to.

Reminds me of a game in which Joe Garagiola was the catcher. He didn't name the pitcher, but Stan Musial came up to bat. Stan was at the top of his game and hitting the ball left and right out of the park. Garagiola called for a fast ball. The pitcher shook his head. Joe called for a curve ball. The pitcher shook it off. He called for the fork ball, the pitcher's specialty. The pitcher shook his head. Joe walked out to the mound and said, "I've called everything in the book; what do you want to throw?" "Nothing," said the pitcher. "I just want to hold on to the ball as long as I can."

My mother, who knew something about this holding on in the depths of her despair. She used to say, "When all reason to be is gone, you've got to keep on keeping on." And that is what the Honduran man was doing. I will think of him often as a symbol of hope.

Hope is the last but not least of the Seven Cardinal Virtues. Hope is faith on its knees. When life gets desperate, hold on to *whatever* as long as you can. If there were no *in the depths,* there would be no need for hope. If all went well all the time there would be no need for hope. If all went well all the time there would be no need for faith or love or the other virtues. Without virtues, the concept of character would be meaningless, and without character we would not be free—we would be robots.

Whatever was, whatever is and whatever will be, is in the inscrutable nature of God. In the end we will discover that everything God did was good. *And then God saw everything he had made and behold it was very good,* [Gen. 1:31] no matter how twisted it seems from our limited human view.

I'm taking off the wings now. You might want to use them to do a bit of flying yourself. It's risky but it can be fun.

You Can't Steal First

There's an old riddle: A man wants to go home but he is afraid. He gets within thirty yards but sees a man wearing a mask waiting there and so he hesitates. Where is he? The answer, of course, is that he is a runner on third base in a baseball game. It is within the rules of baseball that a player, if he is able, can steal home. But also in the rules is "You can't steal first."

Not a single game we play would be fun very long if we bent the rules. I remember the wild games of Monopoly we had when it was in vogue. One of the children would be almost squeezed out of the game and would ask to borrow some money. I wouldn't allow it, and they thought I was mean. What would it hurt just this once? What would hurt is that just this once would become just this twice, etc.

My son, Gerry, liked chess. We played many games. I would never let him win if I could help it. He kept getting better and better but couldn't beat me. He grew up and went to Viet Nam. When he came home he said one day, let's play a game of chess. He beat me fair and square. He'd been practicing. I'm sure it was a proud moment for him and it was for me, too. How much would he have improved if I had made silly moves to let him win. Life has rules and these rules are not silly; they are implicitly necessary for successful group living; they're built in at the factory, so to speak.

Humans have codified these built-in laws—*they only codified, not invented*—the laws. Hammurabi, king of Babylonia, in the 17th century B.C. wrote down what was probably the severest code informed by "an eye for an eye and a tooth for a tooth." Five hundred years later Moses brought down from the mountain the Ten Commandments, a code which has been basic to every other document of freedom. Jesus gave us the Golden Rule: *Do unto others as you would have them do unto you*. One little boy came home from Sunday School and said, "I learned the Golden Rule: Do others before they do you."

Rules are like train tracks. How far would trains get if they found the rails too confining and went off on their own? Our rails are the laws of God and of government. More and more, it seems, Americans are trying to get off the tracks so they can be free.

But what they are really seeking, I believe, is not freedom but to be unbuttoned. When people get off the rails and run around unbuttoned, the results are mostly disastrous.

And there are unwritten rules about sharing, helping and being polite. A seven-year-oldwas eating with his fingers. His mother said, "Eat with your fork, dear." The child said, sassily, "Fingers were made before forks, mother." The wise mother replied, "Not yours, dear."

Social peace and happiness is in direct proportion to the number of people who are "law-abiding citizens." But some will say, "How can I be free if I'm bound by all these rules?" And the answer is: Laws are your guarantee of freedom. They not only limit you, they limit your neighbor. You lose the right to take something that belongs to your neighbor, but at the same time you gain the freedom of ownership. You give up the right to drive on whichever side of the 'road you want, but you gain the relative freedom to drive on one side in safety. Does that make everything clear, Class? Ah, I see someone is holding up his hand. "You have a question, sir?"

"Yes. I resent it when I obey all the rules and somebody else breaks them again and again and is not punished. What can we do about that?"

"Thank you, sir, for that question. Superb question. Yes. It shows an intelligence rarely seen, a breadth of understanding of social issues that's quite rare. Yes. Excellent question. Next question?

The simplistic answer is: Catch all the rascals and inflict the proper punishment. But simplistic propositions mask difficult procedures. A place to start, however, might be to ask whether our plight is due, not to too strict laws, but to too lenient punishments. Maybe Hammurabi went too far with his "You steal orange—I cut off your hand, you walk in forbidden place I cut off your foot, seduce neighbor's wife I cut off your—etc."

Tightening up sentencing, however, might be a place to start. Maybe we ought to look a little harder at Monopoly with its "Go directly to jail. Do not pass go." And maybe also to look at the weakening moral fiber of our country—starting with ourselves. Ask yourself, "What standards am I willing to accept today that yesteryear I would have cried out so vehemently against?" Let me misquote Shakespeare here: *The fault, dear Brutus, is not in our stars, but in ourselves that we are in this mess.*

Maybe we're trying to steal first base.

Where Is God?

Two little boys, eight and ten, mercilessly plagued their family and neighborhood with their pranks. It got so bad the mother, at her wits end, took them to the pastor of their church. She explained her predicament and asked him if he could possibly help. He said he'd try and took the youngest into his study. He put him in a chair and stood over him with a stern face and said: "Where is God?" The child, scared, didn't answer so the question was repeated more loudly: "WHERE IS GOD?" Still no answer so the clergyman Got close, screwed up his face and shouted: "**WHERE IS GOD**?" The boy dashed out of the room, past his mother, and all the way home where he got in a closet and closed the door. The other brother, right behind, flung himself in the closet and said, "What happened?" The younger brother replied, "We're in BIG trouble! God is missing and they think we did it!"

Where is God? is a question an atheist might ask a believer: "If you're so sure God exists, tell me where he is."

According to one atheist, Gherman Titoy, God is not in space. Titoy, one of the early Russian communist astronauts said, "I looked everywhere for God as I circled the earth and he was nowhere to be found." Now the two boys really *are* in trouble—God is not even in space. Kidding aside, such questions as "Where is God?" are like "Where is Mind?"Mind is an intangible concept, incapable of being perceived by the senses. A forensic surgeon might say, "I have taken every bit of a brain apart and nowhere did I find mind." You know there is mind. I know there is mind. We use our minds every living moment. We can't define it nor can we locate it; we just use it. I can't define God. I can't tell you where his central base of operations is—if indeed there is such. But I talk with him and fellowship with him. So do you. As Paul said in his masterful open-air sermon to the philosophers in the Areopagus in Athens *The God who made the World and everything in it is the Lord of heaven and earth and does not live in temples made with hands . . . though he is not far from each one of us. For in him we live and move and have our being.*

Where is God, indeed! When I was five years old I knew that God was in heaven. I didn't know where heaven was except it was somewhere "out there." I knew that Jesus was there and my father who died in the flu epidemic in 1918 was there, too. In fact, I was so sure of this that when we said, "Our Father who art in heaven," I knew we were talking to my father who was up there with God. Children know such things. Like the little girl who told her Sunday School teacher that God was in her bathroom. "Why do you say that, dear?" asked the teacher. "Because," she said, "every morning my father knocks on the bathroom door and says, "My god, are you still in there?"

To my mind the American astronauts who circled the moon some years ago were more "down to earth" about God. They didn't ask where he was; they just talked to him. Unabashedly, before the whole human race, they prayed to him as they whirled through space. This upset another atheist no end. Madalyn Murray O'Hair, registered a protest with NASA, calling the prayer in outer space "a tragic situation." Poor Madalyn! I can see her now, up in God's classroom writing one million times on the blackboard "I will not say, 'there is no God . . . I will not say there is no God . . . I will not say . . .'" I like Gandhi's rejoinder to an atheist. This particular atheist was trying to engage him in a discussion on the existence of God. "It amazes me," Gandhi said, "how much energy you atheists invest in disproving something you don't believe exists in the first place." Amen. Nuff said!

Almost. I ran across an irrefutable answer to the atheist who asks for proof of the existence of God. It concerned one Charles Bradlaugh, England's most notorious atheist (influential in getting swearing on the Bible replaced with affirming, in British courts) and editor of *The National Reformer*. He challenged Hugh Price Hughes, eminently effective evangelist and director of the West London Mission, to a showdown, to prove once and for all that God did not exist. Hughes accepted. In the next issue of the London Times Hughes ran a full page ad describing the challenge. In the ad were listed the names of dozens of people who once were thieves, prostitutes, and drunkards. Each one wrote a brief testimony as to how he or she had found God and how God had lifted them from the gutter and changed them to joyful, working, law-abiding people. On the bottom of the page, in large letters, Hughes threw down the gauntlet: "Mr. Bradlaugh, if you can show me one man or woman who was so dramatically changed by your atheism, I will concede the debate." No more was heard from Bradlaugh.

The proof of the pudding is in the eating. Speaking of which, I must be related to Pooh Bear. My tummy is pulling me toward the fridge. See you later.

The Ten Suggestions

In one of the Frank and Ernest comic strips, Frank and Ernest are in a law library staring at the thousands of volumes lining the walls. Frank says, "It's frightening when you think that all this started with just 10 commandments."

How many people seriously contemplate the Ten Commandments today—not because the Commandments have been tried and found difficult, but because they've been found hard and not tried. The Ten Commandments are by their nature disciplines. All disciplines are hard. A woman calling in to the Claprood and Whitley radio show on RKO the other morning put it quite succinctly: "The young people of my era trashed a whole generation." In the conversation that unfolded she clarified her position with the statement, "My era opted out of the disciplined life."

If we look back a few years we know what she meant. The word discipline comes from the same root as disciple, the Latin root of which means to learn. That generation did not want to learn from those who had gone before. They "opted out." They were like the man who climbed up in a tree to trim some limbs but sat on the very limb he was sawing off at the trunk. The Ten Commandments are the result of long and painful social learning. They were codified by Moses as a guide for his people so they wouldn't make the mistakes which had brought down tribes and kingdoms before them. They are not simply arbitrary rules, they are concise statements of cause and effect. "If you do these things, positive results will follow; if you do not, beware!"

One minister found this out. He decided to preach a series of sermons on the Ten Commandments. Everything went fine until he sat down to write a sermon on the seventh commandment. He let out an expletive and said, "Now I remember where I left that bicycle!"

Actually the Ten Commandments were not a new thing when Moses read them to his people. The Babylonian King, Hammurabi, included all but one of the commandments in his own code of laws (the Hammurabi Code) at least four hundred years before the time of Moses. As is true with most good and effective laws, they are not true because they are proclaimed—they are proclaimed because they are true. One Commandment Moses gave was different—absolutely unique. *I am the Lord thy God . . . Thou shalt have no other gods before me*. This belief was totally without precedent. And there is another commandment a few pages further on, not included with those Moses brought down from Sinai *Thou shalt love thy neighbor as thyself* Leviticus 19:18] without question the most important of all the commandments of Judaism. Jesus quoted it and used it as the watershed between his teachings and the teachings of the Law. These two commandments alone make the Bible a monument of religious insight never before grasped and never since surpassed. The Ten Commandments have been the basis for every great document of freedom devised, including the Magna Carta and the Constitution of the United States. What then should we as individuals, as members of churches and as followers of Jesus, do with these pronouncements that reside in the pages of that book we keep on the shelf? It might be enlightening to make a comparison between the Constitution of the United States and the Ten Commandments.

We note first that the Ten Commandments do not have a preamble, maybe Moses should have written *We, the children of God, in order to establish a more perfect kingdom, insure domestic tranquility, promote the general welfare, and secure the blessings of unity to ourselves and our posterity do ordain and establish these Ten Commandments for the Kingdom of God.*

But composing beautiful prose is the easy part, isn't it? How are the Constitution and the Ten Commandments to be "enforced?" Let's look. Very soon after hammering out the provisions in the Constitution it became necessary to make amendments; and so it was with the Commandments. The Children of Israel soon strayed and it became necessary to create a myriad of lesser laws (see the books of Leviticus and Numbers). How many court cases have tested the meaning of the Constitution's articles and amendments? How many splits have there been in the Kingdom of God because of conflicting interpretations of the Word? Apparently, then, such comparisons are not too helpful. I should throw this section out, but then I'd just have to write something else to fill the space. I have to remind Frank (talking to Ernest, above) that the most important law library that ever existed is in our hearts. Only two laws: The most important one, Jesus said, is this *Hear O Israel, the Lord our God, the Lord is one. Love the Lord your God with all your heart and with all your soul and with all your mind and with all your strength. The second is this: Love your neighbor as yourself There is no commandment greater than these.* And in spite of how mighty and powerful these laws are, they can be broken. Or put more correctly we break ourselves when we disobey them.

A woman was mailing the old family Bible to her brother in another city. The postal clerk asked the usual question, "Does this package contain anything breakable?" "Only the Ten Commandments," the woman answered. When we break these we break not only our own heart but the heart of God. We should all get out these laws and think about them, test our lives against them and begin to reenter the disciplined life.

An editor, tired of the abusive letters he received concerning his daily editorials, one day printed in their place the Ten Commandments and nothing more. A few days later came a letter that read: "Cancel my subscription; you're getting too personal."

I'm sure, knowing y'all, this won't apply to you, but if it does, don't write me. Write to God. He's the author. They're his laws, not mine.

Marriage is a Great Institution . . . .

. . . . if you want to spend your life in an institution. I DIDN'T MAKE IT UP—I'M ONLY QUOTING! Marriage has been forever and it has always been blessed by some sort of ceremony—except the first one. As far as I can tell, Adam and eve never were officially married. Adam probably took some "ribbing" about that. But I got to wondering whether, in our "enlightened" era we have improved on the earlier models of marriage. In ancient Rome the couple were married by the Groom's father, the *patria postestes*, the powerful fathier. After all, he owned his own wife and his children and with this marriage he owned his son's bride, too. Was there an advantage to this? In some ways, yes. One of the advantages was the "bride price." To get this bride for his son, the father had to pay a pretty penny to the brides father who was now losing some of his property. Sounds callous. But wait! If the bride doesn't live up to expectations, she can be returned to her family and her father has to repay the "price" he was paid for her. On the other hand, if she is mistreated by her new husband, she could demand to be returned to her family and her father was not obliged to return the "price" paid for her.

All in favor of returning to that system hold up your ring finger. Seeing none, we'll move right along.

Try this one. In certain Southern Pacific societies a man and woman marry but don't live together. They only visit. He lives with his sister and helps her care for her children (his nephews and nieces). She lives with her brother who helps her take care of her children. Think I saw a couple of ring fingers go up on that one. In spite of the fact that separations were almost non-existent In the above examples of mate selection, I can't imagine our society opting for either of them. Romance undergirds mate selection in our society, which is beautiful and fine as long as we use it for that. There is danger otherwise, like the man who proposed to his fiancee In the car and she accepted in the hospital.

After the honeymoon, when we are dumped into reality, we need something more substantial. That something is most clearly stated in a story I read recently. A young couple was invited forward by the pastor of a mid-western church. They faced the congregation and said, "We are not cheapskates. We simply don't like lavish weddings and costly receptions. Besides, you are our family and it is within this family we hope to establish our own." A three-minute marriage ceremony followed, after which they went out to the coffee hour—their reception.

Sounds to me like the couple married on Gibraltar because as they said, "We wanted our marriage to be solid like a rock." I think the church couple found a better rock, the Rock of Ages.

In one episode of the comic strip **B.C.**, the chief character is looking up the meaning for the word *Bible* in a huge dictionary lying across a rock. The definition he found read ***A word from your sponsor.*** When I saw this cartoon I knew I had to write about it. Some will say the comic strip trivializes the Book of Books. Obviously I Think otherwise. As I grew up the Bible was as much a part of life as meat and water and sunlight. it was like a piece of clothing; you'd be embarrassed to be Bible naked; like the American Express card, no one left home without it. It has only been in the last two decades that I have come to realize that other people were not reared in the same fashion. And in the last few years I have awakened to the abysmal lack of Biblical knowledge in the world. This in spite of the statistic that around ten million bibles are published in 150 countries around the world each year.

Could I be wrong about the importance I have attributed to this *Word From Our Sponsor?* I like the way Immanuel Kant stated it: "Our ultimate purpose in reading the Bible is to make us better men and women." Not perfect men and women . . . . just better. But I knew another purpose in reading this "Manufacturer's Handbook." It was to know my Maker, to understand more clearly my Sponsor, to walk with him and talk with him. There are two ways to read the Bible. One way is to talk to it, tell it what you want it to say. The other is to let the Bible talk to you. To let it inspire you. To let it on occasion lift you from the hard road you tread and put a cushion of air under your feet. The first way is to search for proofs to back up your point of view. The better way is to search for God's point of view to back up your essential reason for being. To read the Bible this way is to read with your critical faculties in neutral and the door of your heart open.

Have a Bible you can make your own—that is, one you can use colored hi-liters in, one you can underline favorite passages in, one you can write in the margins of. Such a Bible becomes your own unique and personal Handbook. I was never so thankful for this as when my Aunt Catherine sent me my father's Bible when I was 21 years of age; he died before I knew him. I went through it and read the underlined passages and felt like I had a message from heaven. Later I received my Grandma Parson's marked up Bible. My grandma must have been the one a Sunday School girl had in mind when the teacher asked, "What is in the Bible?" and she said, "A lock of hair, a pressed flower, a recipe for brownies and a pink ribbon." Gram's Bible was full of such things. A person who grew up in the same denomination I did was Charles Schulz, the creator of Peanuts. This will not surprise you when you recall how often his comics center around the Bible. For instance, We see Charlie brown looking at Snoopy who is sitting on his dog house typing out an essay. He let's Charlie read it. *As it says in the ninth chapter of Ecclesiastes, 'A living dog is better than a dead lion.'*

Charlie says to Snoopy, "What does that mean?"

Snoopy replies, "I don't know but I agree with it."

Which reminds me of one of the first verses I had to memorize as a boy, Ecclesiastes 12:1 *Remember now thy Creator, in the days of thy youth, while the evil days come not, nor the years draw nigh, when thou shalt say, I have no pleasure in them.*"

I agree with it. The years have drawn nigh and I'm glad I remembered when I did.

The Talking Machine

Thomas A. Edison often spoke at conferences. At one such he was introduced to the audience as the inventor of the "talking machine." Mr. Edison rose and began his address as follows: "I must insist on a correction to that gracious introduction. God invented the talking machine. I only invented the first one that can be shut off."

In one of my pastorates, longer ago than I care to remember, there was a lovely woman who was a sterling example of God's "talking machine." I'll call her Mazie. When Mazie was under construction, her on-off switch for talking got stuck in the on position which is to say, she could "talk one's ear off."

Mazie called me at the church study every single day. Like waiting for the other shoe to drop, I'd have my coffee then be restless till that call came, after which I could begin the day. This all came to a head one morning when, leaning back in the desk chair, listening to Mazie, I leaned too far and over I went, the phone flying. I got up and with as much aplomb as possible, suggested to Mazie that she make an appointment when she wanted to talk and then we could enjoy a face-to-face conversation.

I can laugh now at Mazie's many words, but it makes me wonder: what if there were no words? Humans, after all, are the only animals that talk—the only animals that *can* talk—because of a small area in the left hemisphere of our brain. It's called Broca's area, after it's discoverer, Paul Broca.

A French neurologist, anatomist and surgeon of the 19th century, Broca was the founder of modem brain surgery. He discovered the area in the brain that enables us to pronounce words—a monumental achievement. Broca is infamous for a less efficacious pronouncement: "Men are superior to women," a statement so ludicrous I would not stoop so low as to even put into print.

Without the speech area of the brain, life in general would lose its kaleidoscopic nature. Could we communicate with one another at all? I guess so—with body language and grunts—lower animals do. But the quality would be vastly different. We would look about us at trees, houses, rivers, ocean, flowers, sun, etc., and have no words for them; no way to express our feeling about them to another person. Or how about colors, flavors, or feelings? What if nothing had ever been named or ever could be named because our brain had no capacity for naming? There would be no words for love, family, home, work. What would Mazie do? What would this preacher do on Sunday morning? I shudder.

Without Broca's area in the brain, life in various particular ways would lose its ability to thrill, excite, and motivate . . . and of course to appall and disgust, too. Take the area of religion for example. There would be no word for church, God or Jesus. There would be no Bible if there were no words—unthinkable! There would be no hymns if there were no words—unthinkable! There would be no sermons if there were no words.

Well—maybe that's thinkable.

That's why for me, the first verse of the Gospel of John is so hauntingly beautiful—and meaningful. *In the beginning was the word. The word was with God, and the word was God* Put another way, "in the beginning was expression." God "expressed" himself and there was man: Adam. God expressed himself and there was woman: Eve. God expresses himself and there is you and there is me, for he has said through Isaiah, *Fear not for I have redeemed you, I have called you by your* ***name****—you are mine.* I have expressed you.

So, we *are* a word; we are our name. The one word we like to hear more than all other words is our name—unless it is called by the teacher and we are told to stand up and recite. Later in life we will be happy to stand up and recite words in conversations, sermons, opinions and after dinner speeches. We will be talking machines that are difficult to turn off because we love the sound of our own words. And we assume others do too.

One after-dinner speaker was asked by the master of ceremonies, "Shall we let them enjoy their dessert or do you want to start talking now?"

I assume you have enjoyed my words so far and I am going to stop talking so you can go out and get your dessert.

Model Tees, Morse Code and Marriage

When I was seven I was living on the farm with my grandmother and grandfather. Grampa, around fifty years of age, decided it was time to join the age of miracles and so bought a Model-T Ford. Fords had three pedals on the floor, a magneto to create the spark and a crank to get the magneto, the gasoline and the spark to work together—all a very complicated procedure. None of us, I am sure, can imagine the excitement of going from a horse and wagon to this miraculous device, the Ford. It is still exciting, eighty years later, to get a new car, but nothing to match Grampa's enthusiasm.

Or grandma's. Nothing was going to keep her from learning to drive this contraption! She didn't drive it long, however, especially after she couldn't get the Ford stopped one day and drove it on top of the woodpile. She got scratched up getting down and was considerably embarrassed, watching grampa get the car down, muttering something unintelligible under his breath. The thing that really put an end to her driving career, however, was going through the back of the barn when she put the Ford in reverse and couldn't get it to stop until it was in the manure pile.

After that it was Grampa's car. Instead of horse and wagon he drove the Ford back and forth to the railroad yard where he worked. In the days before he owned a car he would finish the day's work, untie the horse, get in the wagon and drive home. Sometimes he would fall asleep, and the horse, knowing the route as well as Grampa did, took him safely to the farm. One evening while driving home in the Ford, Grandpa gave in to this same urge to sleep. He got into an accident and suffered a fractured skull and did not live long. The Ford didn't know the way home as well as the mule did. Beware a sudden change in deeply ingrained habits. As Mark Twain said, "Habit is not to be flung out of the window by any man, but coaxed down-stairs a step at a time." Grampa took too many steps at once, going down the stairs.

Habits are not necessarily bad. They take care of repetitive motions so we don't have to think about them, and thus they save time. Imagine what it would be like if you had to think about each small motion as you opened a door or put on your coat. If you do not believe this, try putting your coat on—other arm first—sometime.

In the twenties "wire services" meant news stories coming in through dots and dashes of the Morse code. Expert reporters had to translate the clicks into dots and dashes, dots and dashes into letters, letters into words and after all that to communicate the results through the keyboard of a typewriter—SIMULTANEOUSLY! This they could do with great expertise and some could even read a book while doing it, and know what the book was about! Habits are behavior without thinking. For the above news reporters this was a blessing, but for Grampa, driving his new Ford, it was fatal. It can go either way.

In marriage such automatic behavior can be hurtful. It's called "taking your partner for granted." One wife, seeking a divorce complained to the judge, "He never says he loves me!" The husband replied, "I told her I loved her at the altar 20 years ago, and I ain't never changed my mind."

In church, "habitual religion" can be good news and bad news. The good news is that it fills the pews on Sunday morning. The bad news is that such people get hardening of the categories. One disgruntled church member came to the pastor's desk complaining about the choir, the Sunday School and the fund drive. The pastor said, "I'm glad you came in. I've made some notes and I'll discuss it with the board. Perhaps we can make some changes."

Banging his fist on the pastor's desk, the upset member roared, "And that's another thing I hate around here, change, change, change!"

Without change there is no growth. Without change there is no excitement. Perhaps we should look at our friendships, our marriages, our jobs and ask ourselves, "In what small way could I change my behavior to make life better?"

One man decided to do this. He had been courting his maid for twenty-nine years and finally decided to propose. He got down on his knees, nervous as a cat in a room full of rocking chairs, and stammered, "Maisie, I think we should get married."

"Me, too, Clem," she answered, "but who would have us?"

O, well! Still worth a try.

Who, Me Scared?

A small boy in the old west was watching a cobbler repair some boots.

"What do you use to fix 'em with?" asked the boy.

"Hide," answered the cowboy.

"What?" said the boy.

"I said hide. You know—the cow's outside," replied the cobbler.

"Heck," said the boy, "I don't care. I'm not afraid of any old cow!"

As you can see, courage means different things to different people. It's a relative term—the more relatives you have the more courage you need. Just kidding! Just kidding!

I've always liked this story from World War I: a charge was in progress, soldiers were rushing forward, bodies bent close to the ground. One soldier stood stock still as other soldiers rushed past him, calling out, "Coward! Coward! Later, at his court martial he said, "If the ones calling me coward were half as scared as I was, they'd have been running toward the rear!" Courage *is* relative and there is no way to quantify it on a scale of 1 to 10. And to confuse matters, there are different kinds of courage.

There is moral courage—the courage of one's convictions—like one of my parishioners in Abington, Massachusetts had. He was asked by his employer to do something he considered unethical. He told him he couldn't do it and why. He was told, "Your convictions are no concern of ours. Either do what I ask or quit." And quit he did, even though he had no savings with which to feed clothe and house is family. This kind of ethical courage seldom makes the news, but physical courage is reported in the media every day. "Man saves boy from drowning, woman rushes into burning building to save child, etc."

And there is spiritual courage, sometimes called faith. Spiritual courage testifies by word and behavior to one's beliefs. There was a little girl having lunch in a diner with her parents. She wanted to say grace, but looked at all the adults at the counter and paused. But having the courage of her convictions she said to her mother, "Shouldn't we say grace?" The mother shushed her, but a burly truck driver overheard the little girl and said in a loud voice, "Every one here bow your head for grace." Every patron did while the little girl prayed:

> With gratitude we bow our head
> To thank thee for our daily bread.
> Amen.

One little act, but we can imagine what it did for those diners that day.

This same kind of courage "grown up" is exemplified in Maxwell Anderson's 1939 drama *Key Largo* about the Spanish Civil War. A small group of American volunteers were fighting to help Spain throw off the yoke of tyranny. They find themselves one night on a ridge which they know they cannot hold very long. But holding it as long as possible would deny the enemy time and make the escape of their comrades more certain. The small group is for leaving—all except Victor who said, "Something in me would perish if I didn't believe that in the world there is a spirit that would rather die than accept injustice." One of his buddies, a cynic, tries to persuade him that political decisions are made by powerful individuals who hide behind their slogans in order to pursue selfish gains and keep common people fighting over empty symbols. "There's nothing to win even if you could win it, he states. Victor replies with these words:

> *Yes, but if I die then I know men will never give in; then I know there is something in the race of men, because even I had it, that hates injustice more than it wants to live—because even I had it—and I'm no hero.*
>
> *And that means the Hitlers and the Mussolinis always lose in the end—force loses in the long run, and the spirit wins, whatever spirit is. Anyway, it's the thing that says it's better to sit here with the moon and hold them off while I can.*
>
> *If I went with you, I'd never know whether the race was turning down again, to the dinosaurs—this way I keep my faith in myself and what men are and what we may be.*

And then there's the courage of hope—hanging on to the belief that God is with us—even when it seems impossible. It is probably the bedrock of all courage. When I see it in action it is one of the wonders of the human world. The other night in class a student was telling some of the horrors of her young life—child abuse—incest. "From the moment it first occurred," she said, "there was a huge hole in my life. It was my childhood. I never really was a child. And since it always happened in the dark, I've been afraid of the dark ever since." After a failed marriage she was left to bring up a child and then she developed cancer and came within a hair of dying. So what did she do? She joined the hospice movement which had been so great helping her through her ordeal. She wanted to help others have the courage—the courage of hope—to face their last days of life.

A small girl wrote a letter to God: "Dear God, sometimes I am very scared in my room at night. But I know you are there. Aren't you? Your friend, Diane."

Yes, Diane, even in the middle of the darkest night he is there. Not only that, but he's got his arms around you.

You Know the Old Saying

Polly and I were visiting church members at the Hale Hospital in Haverhill, Massachusetts. We were asked by a nurse to look in on Henry, third bed on the right. Henry didn't get many visitors. He probably had outlived his friends and family. He was happy to see us—to see anyone for that matter—and tried to show it by keeping up his end of the conversation. There was one thing different about his tete-a-tete, however; he prefaced nearly everything he said with, "You know the old saying."

Old sayings are called cliches, old saws, and bromides (they put one to sleep). Such word constructs are red-penciled by English teachers and book editors because they lack originality. Other "old sayings" are elevated to the level of adages, proverbs and maxims because they embody the wisdom and truths of a society.

The trouble with Henry's "old sayings," however, were that they were none of the above—not even old. He would say, "You know the old saying *It's nice to see you," or* "You know the old saying *I hope I'm going home soon*," or "You know the old saying *Thanks for dropping by*."

As we walked away I said to Polly, "There's a sermon there somewhere." I felt sorry about Henry's desperate attempt to be, you know the old saying, *One of the crowd, a regular guy.* I felt guilty about smiling at his "old sayings." But now I am paying homage to the talkative stranger who was, well you know the old saying, *A real sweetheart.*

It seems odd we can't use old sayings in formal writing yet can't get along without such verbal shorthand in conversation. If we eliminated all the old sayings from everyday language, we'd never finish a conversation. But there are comics who make a living by putting a twist on old sayings. A few examples:

> The oboe is an ill wind that nobody blows good.
> All work and no play make jack.
> Where is a will there is a bunch of relatives.
> The course of two loves never runs smooth.
> Father is the kin you love to touch.
> Clothes fake the man.

Humorists do the same thing. A humorist is a comedian who takes longer to tell his jokes. Here's one by that accomplished humorist James Thurber. He uses one hundred and fifty words to turn an old saying into a story.

Two men were walking across an open field carrying a huge pane of glass. A sparrow, unable to see the glass, flies right into it and falls stunned to the ground. Soon another sparrow does the same thing. When they come to, one sparrow says to the other, "Let's go back and tell the flock back there. They'll never believe it!" So they did, saying to their fellow sparrows, "You wouldn't believe what happened to us today! We were flying across the meadow over yonder when suddenly the air solididied right in front of us and knocked us out cold." The other birds pooh-poohed the story, saying, "That's scientifically impossible. Air doesn't solidify." Nevertheless they decided to fly over and view the scene of the miracle. They decided to prove their conviction to the "injured" sparrows. "We'll fly right where you did just to show you." One after another the sparrows flew with all their might across the field, only to hit the glass and fall stunned to the ground. The last sparrow "chickened out" and didn't fly across the field. All of which goes to prove the old saying *He who hesitates is not always lost.* The largest repository of old sayings is, of course, the Bible. The following are probably familiar to you:

> Spare the rod and spoil the child.
> A soft answer turns away wrath.
> Pride goes before a fall.
> Don't put your lamp under a bushel.

This last "old saying" was understood perfectly by Jesus' listeners. The lamps of that day were simply wicks floating on oil in a gravy boat. The lamp was kept on a lamp stand. With no matches or Zippo lighters in those days, lamps were not easy to light, so when they went out they put a bushel-sized container over the lamp to protect the flame till they returned. Jesus was saying to his followers, "You have received my light, but it does no good if it is hidden. *Let your light so shine before men that they may see your good works and give glory to your father who is in heaven.*"

Sometimes I'm a bit slow in following Jesus' dictums. How about you? We act like we've got all the time in the world. Maybe we'd better listen to the ants in the following story.

A duffer on the golf course kept missing his drive but digging up clouds of dirt, including an ant hill. One ant said to the other, "If we are going to keep on living, we'd better—you know the old saying—get on the ball."

And now—you know the old saying—It's time for me to wrap it up. Ta-ta.

Expectations

In Bill Waterson's cartoon strip, Calvin and Hobbes, we see Calvin and Susie in an elementary school classroom. They just got their test papers handed back by the teacher. Calvin says to Susie, "What grade did you get"

"I got an A."

"Really?" says Calvin, "I'd hate to be you. I got a C.

"Why on earth would you rather get a C than an A?"

"I find my life is a lot easier the lower I keep everyone's expectations."

From the Latin *spectare* (look) plus the *ex* (out) we get *to look out for or to look for "especially."* Calvin wouldn't mind people simply looking at him, but to look for him to be especially smart or extra good or something, that would upset him. Another way he could have said the same thing: "I just want to be *normal*."

Sixty-eight percent of the population are "normal." That means they occupy the "middle" of the normal curve (the bell-shaped curve). That leaves sixteen percent who are "higher"on the scale and sixteen percent who are "lower," whatever "higher" and "lower" mean. This fact has always astounded me. Whatever trait is being measured—height, beauty, intelligence, athletic ability, wealth, whatever—the normal curve always comes out the same. There are sixty-eight percent who will fall in the middle of the curve. I used to believe that someday I would get a class of all A students but it never happened. The largest number always got Cs, the next largest number got either Bs or Ds and the smallest number got As or Fs. After twenty-six years I've given up. The normal curve is here to stay.

When the Chief of Chaplains (a major general) addressed us newly commissioned chaplains, he said, "Twenty percent of the soldiers you serve will be so good you can do nothing to improve them; twenty percent will be so bad you can't help them; so work on the sixty percent in the middle. I'm not sure Jesus would have operated on that principle. He might have gone directly to the hopeless, but then none of us was a Jesus.

This was true in the churches I served, too. There were always a few wet blankets who (like the chaplain said) could not be helped in any way. They are the "pillars" of the church (they hold up progress). Then there were those gems always ready to do their bit; the ones who made the church hum and zip. The rest were necessary; they helped fill the pews on Sunday. The people who know most about the psychology of church membership, the professional fund-raisers, have a law: *eighty percent of the budget will always be pledged by twenty percent of the members*! No good to cry, "Get the one-dollar-pledgers to up their giving." Save your breath, dig down and increase your own pledge.

Why so many "average" people? I don't know, but let it be said, the normal curve pattern is so universal it has to be a part of God's plan. You've heard the aphorism *God must love the common man; he made so many of them;* and if you think about it, you can see the wisdom. What if everyone could play baseball as well as Ted Williams or paint as well as Michelangelo or sing as well as Pavaroti? Who would be left to sit in the bleachers or go to art galleries or the opera? As one baseball manager put it, "There are plenty of people better at baseball than Ted Williams; I just can't get them to come down out of the stands." If everyone could do everything as well as everyone else, the normal curve would be a flat line, and "flat" is the operative word here. Life would be flat. So I guess Susie should thank Calvin and all the other C students for their modest ambitions. Otherwise what meaning would her A have? It seems inevitable that there be the Calvins of this world who simply want to remain anonymous in some regard. Like the man who had his name legally changed from Pulaski to Kelly. Two years later before the same judge he changed to Finklestein. Two years after that he changed to Garibaldi. The judge glared and inquired, "Sir, are you trying to make a fool out of me?" "Oh, no sir," said the man. "It's just that my neighborhood keeps changing." Calvin would understand that.

I guess being normal isn't so bad, especially if you are talking to the man in the white coat!

Political Incorrectness

Seventy-two years ago a brown-haired, brown-eyed boy, was holding hands with a black-haired, blue-eyed girl. He said, "Will you marry me when we grow up?" She said she would. So to seal the bargain, the boy took off his jacket, put it over their heads and in that secrecy and darkness they sealed the promise with a kiss. I was that little brown-eyed boy my fiance was Gertrude.

If that incident happened today, Duane would be suspended from school on the grounds of harassment, or political incorrectness. just as Jonathan Prevette of Lexington North Carolina was. Like me, Jonathan was six years old, and he too kissed a girl on the cheek, only he was kicked out of school on the grounds of "inappropriate behavior." Jonathan's girl friend *asked* him to kiss *her*; I did it without being asked. If one of us should have been kicked out of school for political incorrectness, it was I. But I was only doing what Jesus taught *Do unto others as you would have them to do unto you.*

And talk about being politically incorrect! My classroom misbehavior did not end with simply kissing a girl. Goodness sakes no! I used to take the pigtail of the girl in front of me and dip it in my inkwell. Talk about your "bad hair days!"

All this took place in a one-room red school house with six grades and one teacher. Having only outdoor plumbing—a three-holer. The teacher had to monitor the goings of the children who held up one finger or two fingers. I always wondered what difference there was in one finger or two. If you gotta go, you gotta go, and how did she know whether you held up one finger but actually did two—maybe even both? Life was complicated in those days. I suppose political incorrectness in such a pressure cooker takes on a whole new meaning for a teacher. Maybe that's why a switch or a paddle was necessary back then.

One time I got caught scratching initials in the desk top—damaging public property. Without a fair trial, I was spanked with a paddle. And to add insult to injury, the paddle I was spanked with was one I had brought to the teacher to use on the "really" bad kids. Now I was the first one to be spanked with it. Today that teacher would have been fired on the spot for child abuse. Just kidding! I actually believe in spanking. If my mother found out about my indiscretion in school, she was apt to lay one on me, too. She had the cute trick of making me go out and find the switch I was to be punished with. It has been said, and probably correctly, "Everything else in the modern home is controlled by the flick of a switch—why not the children?"

By today's standards, I guess I was abused by both parents and teachers. I wonder what heights I might have risen to had it not been for all that damage to my ego.

Expulsion from school was rare in those days, though it did happen to one little girl. Everything was quiet one day when we heard a tinkle-tinkle-tinkle and a yellow pool accumulated under the chair of this first-grader. She was removed from school till such a time as she understood proper toilet manners and the one and two finger language. Or you might say in today's lingo, till she learned to be politically correct.

Is it not in the same political vein that today some schools ban books like *Huckleberry Finn* from their libraries in elementary schools? Instead of after-the-fact punishment for political incorrectness, our fearless leaders seek prevention of its occurrence by sanitizing library reading lists. Why *Huckleberry Finn*? Because Huck was abused by his alcoholic father? Because a black man and a white boy consorted on a raft-ride down the river? Because of the seamy social ills Huck became aware of at the various stops along the river? Although the slave was captured (I so wanted him to get away) Huck managed a kind of personal freedom. When Tom Sawyer's aunt Sally wanted to adopt Huck, he opted out, afraid that he might become (as he puts it) "sivilized," and he headed west. What are the librarians fearful of? Only God knows, and I'll bet he isn't laughing about it.

If suspending Jonathan and banning *Huckleberry Finn* are examples of a maturing civilization, I think I'd rather head west with Huck.

Human Relations

A freshman after her first day at college wrote home to her parents: "I have decided to major in public relations." In three days her father showed up in his truck. "Pack your things," he said, "you're going home."

"Why, Daddy?" she said through her tears.

"Well, I know what relations is," he said, "and I know what public means. No daughter of mine is going to engage in that kind of stuff."

It is easy to get confused about the meaning of a word like *relations*. It has too many definitions. We have relations (relatives), we relate to animals (birds, cats, horses, dogs). Some say that the dog is man's best friend—especially the hot dog—the only animal that feeds the hand that bites it. Some people have a relationship with Mother Nature. One of my best friends in college (named one of my kids after him) would hug trees in the springtime. But I want to talk about *human* relations, serious human relationships.

Just what is human relations? It is the invisible connection that ties one individual with another, or individuals to others, as in families. It's what makes best friends "best." It's the "bliss" in marital bliss. It's what makes army buddies "bud."

Social psychologists have been trying for years to identify the glue that binds individuals and close-knit groups together. They haven't identified it yet, but they can tell when it is there and what some of the things are that weaken or enhance it.

One of my favorite courses to facilitate was called Human Relations. I say facilitate instead of taught because one cannot teach human relations. It comes close to the true meaning of education (to *educe* or *draw out*). I attempted to educe the possibilities for relationship, but the actual creation of relationships had to be done by the students.

It was one of the most magical courses ever—for me *and* the students. No one ever wanted the course to end and forever after, when one class member encountered another—wherever it might me—they called out their name with a special warm feeling in their heart. What happened in that class to give rise to such a closeness of relationship?

One thing was knowledge. A big block to relationships is lack of real knowledge of each other. We tend to wrap a cloak of privacy around ourselves. We let out only the "safe"stuff like soldiers give out only name, rank and serial number. We have learned that *what they don't know can't hurt us.* To experiment with this we paired off. I say "we" because if I was lucky, there would be an odd number of students and I got to pair off with one of them. A lot of time was spent pairing off and interviewing each other in depth. Every once in a while I would announce, "Introduction Time" and the pairs would tell the class what they had learned about each other, adding some insights that surprised the one being introduced.

This exercise taught us that bias, prejudice and misunderstandings are caused mostly by what we *don't* know about others, and, of course, by what we *think* we know but which turns out to be false.

Following this part of the course was the "Three Knows" exercise which encompasses the totality of knowledge we have about ourselves. 1) What you and I both know about me, 2) What I know about me that you don't, and 3) What you know about me that I don't. This one was usually quite a revelation. I led the way. "One, you and I know that I am a man, a teacher, etc. Two, I know about me but you didn't, that I grew up without a father or a grandfather. And Three, the hard part. I'm going to wait till one of you tells me something about me that I don't know." After a long silence in one class a student held up his hand and said, "On the first day of class you came to class with one brown shoe and one black shoe." They all nodded and began to laugh. I said, "See how our mutual knowledge has grown. Now we are going to do this for each other." The class went by too fast that night and often went overtime.

"Is it not possible," they wanted to know, "to reveal too much about ourselves. Of course, but we all have a natural control valve regulated by the amount of trust developed between us. There are a few people, though, like the boy talking with his date. "I have talked enough about me. Why don't *you* talk about me for a while." Probably their last date.

Deeper relationships are therapeutic. Churches foster such relationships, probably why one historian wrote, "How those Christians love one another!" Probably why church goers live longer than others. Might not Jesus have said *A new command I give you: know one another as I have known you, for by this all men will see that you are my disciples—that you love one another.*

Think I'll pause here, go out and ask Polly to tell me something I don't know about myself. On the other hand, maybe I'd better let sleeping dogs lie.

Fixers and Complainers

In Bill Watterson's comic strip "Calvin and Hobbes" Calvin is having a philosophical discussion with his stuffed tiger, Hobbes as they roll down the hill in their little red wagon. Calvin says, "When I grow up, I'm not going to read the newspaper and I'm not going to follow complex issues and I'm not going to vote. That way I can complain that the government doesn't represent me. Then, when everything goes down the tubes, I can say the system doesn't work, thereby justifying my further lack of participation."

"An ingeniously self-fulfilling plan," says Hobbes, the tiger.

"Yeah," says Calvin, "It's a lot more fun to blame things than fix them."

The word *complain* originally meant to mourn, to beat the breast. Today it means to criticize things or cast blame. I suppose Calvin is right in his assessment of life: *It's a lot more fun to blame things than fix them.* And Calvin is not alone. If you listened to people in groups chatting, you would find that there is hardly a social problem that these plaintive pundits don't have the answer to. I have a theory about why people in groups are more critical than creative: *it takes thinking to be creative and thinking is not compatible with group chit-chat.* Or take a step up to the committee level. Even on this level thinking comes hard. Test this out. The next time you attend a committee meeting propose a new idea and compare the number of criticisms to the thoughtful comments. Maybe the adage is true: "There has never been a monument erected to a committee."

Someone has said, "You know when a person is dead because there's no more complaining." An undertaker inadvertently proved this point when he bought a second-hand station wagon to use as his "courtesy car." The dealer later asked him how it worked out and he said, "Well, I used to get protests from the passengers because of the rough ride, but then I started using it as a hearse and haven't had any complaints since."

I don't want to be too hard on the grousers, because I do a bit of it myself. When I strike up a conversation with someone in a store or the gas station, I'm just as likely to complain about the weather, the economy, the Red Sox, etc. as the next guy. After all, if I were to try being creative and say something like, "You know, if the congress and the president would look at the world situation in light of the holographic theory as espoused by the physicist, David Bohm, maybe they would come up with some innovative international planning," they would look at me in a weird way and walk away. So, being too smart for that, I save my creativity for Sunday morning and a captive audience.

There is certainly much to complain about in the world, maybe more today than ever before—I don't know—but every complaint is also an opportunity to fix something. If I change one word in a little song we sing it would say it all: "It is better to light just one little candle than to *grumble* in the dark."

Reminds me of a young man I knew when I was just out of high school in Washington, D.C. He was a member of our church. His name was John and he came from Greece. He worked in a restaurant and was quite poor. We went out to eat together one Sunday after church. When lunch was over he asked me if I would like to go with him to deliver a package. It was a new shirt he had bought for a boy in a poor family he knew. He might have needed the shirt more than that boy did. I don't remember John's last name or much else about him, but that example of love I never forgot.

We can't solve all the complex issues, Calvin, but as you get older you might discover a deeper kind of fun in fixing just one small bit of the world's brokenness.

Splitting Hairs

A fisherman home from the lake stood in the doorway, lure-lined hat on, tackle box in one hand and in the other, a pole from which was dangling a three-pound fish. "Ta-da!" he said, "look at the fish your old hubby caught!"

"John!" exclaimed his wife, her eyes popping,. "I'm proud of you!"

John had been on the lake since before dawn. He actually caught nothing. On the way home, he stopped by the fish market and bought this sizeable fish. He said to the clerk, "Wait," and he walked away a couple of yards. "Throw it," he said. The clerk did and John caught it and took it home to his wife.

Now what do we call John's statement to his wife? One thing to call it is *splitting hairs*. What John said (I caught this fish) was true; what his wife heard (John caught this fish from the lake) was not true.

Antonio Gauin wrote a book in 1691, *Observations on a Journey to Naples*. In it he spoke of some learned scholastics who became "very dextrous" in presenting proofs by "splitting hairs." The apt phrase became imbedded in many languages. It paints a vivid picture of a barber with a razor, holding a hair up to the light and attempting to split it. Impossible in those days but easily done today with laser light and microscopes.

It is reminiscent of Jesus, poking fun at the Pharisees, with his word picture of a man gagging while attempting to swallow a gnat, but finding no trouble at all swallowing a camel whole. Both epigrams have to do with the truth, the *whole truth* and *nothing but* the *truth*. No splitting hairs.

Do we as Christians have a stand to take on this? I think so. Listen to this excerpt from a great Biblical story, subject of novels and movies, and included in every Bible story book: *Now Joseph was well-built and handsome, and after a while his master's wife took notice of Joseph and said, "Come to bed with me!" But he refused. "With me in charge," he told her, "my master does not concern himself with anything in the house; everything he owns he has entrusted to my care. No one is greater in this house than I am. My master has withheld nothing from me except you, because you are his wife. How then, could I do such a wicked thing and sin against God?" [Genesis 3 9:6-9 NIV]*

Joseph was not always so high-minded and blame free. He had been an irritating person, vain, self-absorbed. But in the old days he was oblivious to his own shortcomings. If his brothers hated him, it was—as far as he was concerned—due to the fact that they were hateful persons. After being sold into Egypt he had no one to turn to for succor and advice but himself and God. He was as alone as a man could get. But it forced him to begin to think and his thinking changed his prayers from "Change my family, change my brothers, change my circumstances," to "Change me, Lord."

That is what all who would climb to greatness must pray: "I acknowledge my transgressions, cleanse me from my sin. Change me, O God, for I am nothing without you." This is the basis for Christian humility and Christian strength: *I am weak but thou art strong, Jesus keep me from all wrong* the hymn says.

It would have been so easy for Joseph to quibble, to split hairs. "She needs me; I am the loneliest of men; I need intimacy; I need a woman's breast to lean on; I have needs which cry out to be satisfied, her desire and my need are natural gifts of God, if my master's wife asks, how can I decline, and think of the power a liaison with the queen would ensure," and on and on—endless rationalizations—endless splitting hairs. Put all these things together—sex, passion, romance, a man's secret hunger for a woman's solace, calculations of advantage, an alibi for conscience—and you have a net of temptation that took great moral strength to not break.

Change names and places and what Joseph faced can essentially be repeated in every generation. It is easy to find excuses for defeat; not so easy to find the strength to prevail.

A husky old priest, whose ministry was mostly among sailors, met one day a man in public life who had got himself involved in a corrupt entanglement. When the priest rebuked him, he said, "But father, you don't realize the strength of the outside pressures on me."

"Outside pressure!" came the indignant reply. "Outside pressure! Where were your inner braces?"

In essence, splitting hairs can only proceed when there is absence of respect for the other person—even God. And how we respect God is reflected in how we respect others. As Joseph said, *How can I do this great wickedness and sin against God?*

Endings and Beginnings

It was the last service of the year for the "Singing Church" at Hampton Beach, New Hampshire. One of the worshipers shook hands at the door and said, glumly, "I hate endings."

"How about beginnings," I said.

"Oh, I love beginnings," she replied.

"Well, there's no ending without a beginning," I said, and left her to think about that if she was of a mind.

Life is one long series of beginnings and endings from the ending of our tenancy in the bathysphere of the womb to the beginning of our bright-light, buttock-slapping, towel-roughing doctor-poking cold-air existence.

Life will teach each of us that the word *beginning* has no meaning without the word *ending* and vice versa. But not all endings are bad and not all beginnings are good. Kids know the difference between good beginnings and bad beginnings—Christmas morning versus school day morning, for instance. Beginning a school day is sometimes an unhappy event, as in the following case.

She went into the bedroom and said, "Get up! It's time for school."

"I don't want to go to school."

"You have to go to school."

"I don't want to—none of the kids like me."

"I Don't care. You have to go to school."

"None of the teachers like me, either."

"I don't care! You're the principal and you have to get up and go to school!"

So, acknowledging the inevitability of good and bad beginnings, what will be our modus operandi? First of all let us concede that the author of the negative-positive aspect of beginning-ending-beginning-ending is God. Secondly, God does not do things willy-nilly. Beginnings and endings are a purposeful gift from God—though often we cannot see the "gift."

Genesis has been called the "Book of Beginnings." And it would appear that at first God was interested only in beginnings; that endings came as an afterthought. Could it be that God was so taken up with the fun of beginnings that he forgot about endings? Do you think God, when he put a big sign DO NOT EAT THIS FRUIT on the apple tree, did not know the devastating effects of temptation? He acted surprised when he said to Adam *Because you followed your mate's suggestion and ate fruit I commanded you not to eat, cursed shall be the ground through you. In suffering shall you gain your living from it as long as you live.* In one fell swoop the free rent and free food were taken away.

Beginnings and endings are parts of God's nature; that is, the pain, joy and mystery of endings and beginnings are resolved in the very being of God. Beginnings and endings, therefore are neither good nor bad; they just are, and because they were given by God [let us make man in our own image], their value and meaning for us are measured by our commitment to him. In both our beginnings and our endings God will be there if we love him. *We know that in everything God works with those who love him.* [Rom. 8:28]

This is why Ira Stamphill could write his great hymn

> Many things about tomorrow I don't seem to understand;
> But I know who holds tomorrow, And I know who holds my hand.

Mary, Queen of Scots, knew as much about endings and beginnings, both happy and tragic, as anyone in history. She had a motto: In my end is my beginning. I believe she was speaking about life's ending and heaven's beginning. The biggest ending of all, death, is the beginning which Jesus described: *There are many rooms in my Father's house; if there were not, I would have told you, for I am going away to make ready a place for you* [John 14:2] That's the beginning all our earthly beginnings and endings are about.

I love the spirit of an elderly church member who called her pastor to her deathbed. "I called you," she said, "because I have a request which I believe you will carry out for me. I can't trust anyone else to do it for sure." She handed him a fork. "That's a dessert fork," she said, "and I want it placed in my casket."

"Please explain," said her pastor."

"Well," she said, "God has been with me in the hard places and easy places of my life. He has led me through the green pastures and beside the still waters and prepared a meal for me in the presence of my enemies. This fork is a symbol of the dessert that awaits me when I go, and I can't wait to get to it!"

I'm not in that big of a hurry. I'll hang on to my dessert fork a little longer. But since this is the last letter I will be writing to you, I would like to close it with the title of my last homily:

Don't cry because it's over—
Smile because it was.